BOBBED

WIVES, and WOMEN

PREACHERS

SIGNIFICANT QUESTIONS FOR HONEST CHRISTIAN WOMEN SETTLED BY THE WORD OF GOD

By
JOHN R. RICE

Evangelist, Founder of THE SWORD OF THE LORD, Author of *The King of the Jews, Prayer—Asking and Receiving, "What Must I Do to Be Saved?" The Home: Courtship, Marriage and Children, The Power of Pentecost, All About Christian Giving, What Is Wrong With the Movies? When a Christian Sins, Revival Appeals,* etc., etc.

SWORD of the LORD
PUBLISHERS
P.O. BOX 1099, MURFREESBORO, TN 37133

Printed in U.S.A.

DR. AND MRS. JOHN R. RICE AND DAUGHTERS

Seated left to right: Joy (Mrs. Roger Martin), Dr. and Mrs. Rice, Joanna (Mrs. Billy Carl Rice). Standing left to right: Jessie (Mrs. Don Sandberg), Mary Lloys (Mrs. Charles Himes), Elizabeth (Mrs. Walter Handford), and Grace (Mrs. Allan MacMullen).

DEDICATED TO MY BELOVED WIFE
AND SIX DAUGHTERS, MY JOY
AND COMFORT AND PRIDE

TABLE OF CONTENTS

authority over men. Based on fundamental differences in man and woman since creation. Women permitted to teach younger women, to teach children, to win souls, but to be in silence as far as teaching men or the whole church, or having any place of authority over men or over the church. Pastors have authority from God to rule, so no woman could be a bishop or pastor. Evangelists were to "command and teach," so Bible forbids woman to be evangelist. I Corinthians 14:34, 35 commands women to be silent in the church. Addressed to all Christians everywhere, therefore binding today. Women forbidden to have authority in the church, likewise commanded to be silent in other mixed gatherings, as far as official teaching or preaching is concerned. There were no women pastors, evangelists, Bible teachers or preachers in New Testament times. Prophetesses were never preachers, never addressed public assemblies. Prophecy is not preaching in Old Testament or New Testament. The case of Agabus. Mistakes of the Scofield Reference Bible. What Acts 2:17, 18 means. Deborah did not preach. Prophetesses obeyed the command to be silent in the church. Arguments for women preachers answered: "Have done so much good," "Women say they are called to preach," "Unfair discrimination," "Women missionaries."

Bible has only incidental teaching about women's clothes, or to be modest. Lipstick, rouge, painted fingernails not expressly forbidden, but seem worldly. But on bobbed hair the Bible is very clear. I Corinthians 11:3-9 examined. Men and women are not alike physically or mentally. A sin for women to be masculine, men effeminate. Why men should wear short hair, take off hats for prayer and worship. New Testament ceremonial symbols with rich spiritual meaning: baptism, the Lord's Supper, laying on of hands, and short hair for men, long hair for women, commanded. Christian women should wear long hair "because of the angels." How bobbed hair might tempt angels to unforgivable sin of rebellion. Long hair, the glory of a woman. What masculine, rebellious women have lost—the respect and reverence of men. Long hair for little girls, too. "If any man seem to be contentious." Excuses answered.

The subject not primarily the hair, but the heart. Appeal to men as well as women. Face the question of surrender to Gods' will and authority. Learn to be subject in homes, schools, churches, business, government. Surrender to the will of God. Not too much, considering what Christ has done for you. Decision slip for sinners. Surrender to Christ.

CHAPTER I

A CONTROVERSY AND HOW TO SETTLE IT

Here are three controversial subjects: (1) Is it a sin for women to cut their hair? (2) Must a wife be subject to, obedient to her husband, ruled by him? (3) Does God ever call or consent for women to be preachers, pastors or evangelists?

The questions are controversial, so weak and fearful preachers avoid these questions. Indifferent Bible students laugh these questions away as of no importance. Many prefer to go by modern opinion without searching the Scriptures. Yet these questions are dealt with so specifically in the Bible and are given such importance that they reach to the very heart of what is wrong with individuals, homes and churches.

These questions can be settled by the Bible, and they cannot be settled in any other way. If you believe the Bible and are willing to listen to what God has plainly said, the writer earnestly believes you can have these questions settled in head and heart by one careful study of this book with an open Bible and one session in the secret closet with God. For the Bible speaks on these matters; it speaks so clearly any honest heart can learn what is God's will. It speaks too definitely to be misunderstood. If you accept the Bible as the authoritative Word of God and are willing to commit yourself wholly to the will of God as expressed in His Word, you may receive great blessings from the study of these questions.

A very prominent preacher said to me once, "John, you are foolish to waste time on a subject like that. Women are not going to pay any attention to you about bobbed hair or the way they dress. You are wasting your breath." But that man was mistaken. There are still many good Christian women who want to do right and who are willing to follow the truth if preachers plainly show them the truth in the Bible. And I have proved it. Literally hundreds of women now have long hair as a result of hearing me teach and preach what God's Word says on that subject. Broken homes have been reunited as rebellious wives learned what God's Word has to say about a woman's submission to her husband and surrender to the will of God. Women have given up large mixed Bible classes, refusing to teach men after they learned that it was plainly forbidden in the Word of God.

I have learned not to be afraid to teach and preach anything that is in the Bible. The Bible works. It still has all the power it ever had. "Is not my word like as a fire? saith the Lord; and like a hammer that breaketh the rock in pieces?" (Jer. 23:29). It is still true that "the word of God is quick, and powerful, and sharper than any twoedged sword, piercing even to the dividing asunder of soul and spirit, and of the joints and marrow, and is a discerner of the thoughts and intents of the heart" (Heb. 4:12).

Those who approach this subject, knowing already all there is to be known and unwilling to be taught, will not learn anything. Those who do not believe the Bible or will not accept its authority might as well mark the Scripture passages given herein and cut them out of their Bibles. If you do not believe God's Word and are not willing to submit to it, you are as guilty as King Jehoiakim of Judah who cut the Word of God with a penknife and then burned the roll in the fire on the hearth (Jer. 36:23). Real modernism does not start on the question of believing in the inspiration of the Bible and the deity of Christ, but in rebellion against the commands of God. Modernism, infidelity, begins not in the head but in the heart. Modernism does not begin first in theology, but in living, not in preaching but in practice! However, if you are willing to accept the Word of God, and acknowledge the authority of Jesus Christ and humbly try to submit yourself to His will wherever He leads you, then you may find a real blessing from this book.

Yes, these are matters of controversy, whether a woman sins in cutting her hair, whether a woman must be subject to her husband, ruled by him, or be equal with him in authority, and whether a woman may be permitted to take the place of authority and leadership in church affairs just as men do, to be a pastor or evangelist. These are controversial matters. But note this, that the controversy is never about *what the Bible says on these questions.* There is no controversy there, for the Bible is so plain that there can be no dispute. The only dispute is whether or not the Bible means what it says, or whether what the Bible says can be binding in this modern day. Bible-believing Christians ought to take what the Bible says to settle these questions.

CHAPTER II

CHRISTIANS TO SUBMIT TO AUTHORITY OF DIVINELY APPOINTED LEADERS IN CHURCH, HOME AND STATE

We call your attention to 1 Corinthians, chapter 11, verses 1 to 16 as a basis for the study of *Bobbed Hair, Bossy Wives and Women Preachers.*

"1 Be ye followers of me, even as I also am of Christ.

"2 Now I praise you, brethren, that ye remember me in all things, and keep the ordinances, as I delivered them to you.

"3 But I would have you know, that the head of every man is Christ; and the head of the woman is the man; and the head of Christ is God.

"4 Every man praying or prophesying, having his head covered, dishonoureth his head.

"5 But every woman that prayeth or prophesieth with her head uncovered dishonoureth her head: for that is even all one as if she were shaven.

"6 For if the woman be not covered, let her also be shorn: but if it be a shame for a woman to be shorn or shaven, let her be covered.

"7 For a man indeed ought not to cover his head, forasmuch as he is the image and glory of God: but the woman is the glory of the man.

"8 For the man is not of the woman; but the woman of the man.

"9 Neither was the man created for the woman; but the woman for the man.

"10 For this cause ought the woman to have power on her head because of the angels.

"11 Nevertheless neither is the man without the woman, neither the woman without the man, in the Lord.

"12 *For as the woman is of the man, even so is the man also by the woman; but all things of God.*

"13 *Judge in yourselves: is it comely that a woman pray unto God uncovered?*

"14 *Doth not even nature itself teach you, that, if a man have long hair, it is a shame unto him?*

"15 *But if a woman have long hair, it is a glory to her: for her hair is given her for a covering.*

"16 *But if any man seem to be contentious, we have no such custom, neither the churches of God.*"

Many other Scriptures will be used, but we will turn again and again to this passage, and it is important that you study it prayerfully.

A QUESTION OF AUTHORITY

In introducing the subject of why Christian women should have long hair and why short hair is a shame for a woman, the Holy Spirit has Paul first to state his authority. The first two verses in the chapter say:

"*Be ye followers of me, even as I also am of Christ. Now I praise you, brethren, that ye remember me in all things, and keep the ordinances, as I delivered them to you.*"

Politically it is the American creed that all men are created free and equal. That is politically true and legally true. Every man must have the same rights before the law. In many spiritual matters men are alike. All alike have sinned, and all alike may be saved by the blood of Christ. God is no respecter of persons in such matters.

But this political creed is not true in other matters. Men are not equal in talents, not equal in opportunities, not equal in responsibilities. Most of all, men are not equal in authority. They ought not to be and cannot be. Here we are plainly told that there is a divine order among Christians. Paul followed Christ, and other Christians should follow Paul. The apostles were called and empowered and given authority that other church members at Corinth did not have. Paul simply commanded, without any false modesty, that Christians were to follow him as he followed Christ.

They were commended when they remembered Paul in all things and kept the ordinances as he delivered them. Paul had authority from God over Christians at Corinth and elsewhere.

This apostolic authority is made plain many times in the Bible. Note how the apostles gathered together to decide the will of God about whether Gentile converts must be circumcised and keep the ceremonial law as recorded in Acts 15, and notice how they gave plain "sentence" (v. 19), "commandment" (v. 24), "burden" (v. 28). Peter in Acts 10:48 "*commanded* them to be baptized." That is the voice of authority, the authority of God. Likewise Paul sent "*a commandment* unto Silas and Timotheus for to come to him with all speed" (Acts 17:15). It is obvious that in the churches others were not equal to the apostles. The apostles exercised authority and ruled over the churches as men with commissions from God.

But preachers, pastors and elders have authority still over churches. To the Hebrews, the Holy Spirit inspired the Apostle Paul to write:

"*Obey them that have the rule over you, and submit yourselves: for they watch for your souls, as they that must give account, that they may do it with joy, and not with grief: for that is unprofitable for you*" (Heb. 13:17).

These "that have the rule" over the Christians, are their spiritual advisers and pastors, watching for their souls, since preachers must give an account to God for their people! Godly pastors are not to be overlords for selfish purposes nor for filthy lucre, we are warned, but they are to "rule" over Christians in the churches, and you Christians in the churches are to "obey them that have the rule over you and submit yourselves." So every pastor, then, might say with Paul, "Be ye followers of me, even as I also am of Christ" (I Cor. 11:1). Hebrews 13:24 says again: "Salute all them that have the rule over you, and all the saints." And other such terms are used more than once in the Bible, teaching that Christians are to be subject to the rulers God put in the church, following these leaders, these overseers, these shepherds, as they follow Christ.

Thus, the question in this chapter, I Corinthians 11, is a question of divine authority.

There is a divine order throughout human society. And we must accept it as true that a certain order of authority and obedience to that authority are the plan of God.

For instance, concerning government, Romans 13:1, 2 says: "Let every soul be subject unto the higher powers. For there is no power but of God: the powers that be are ordained of God. Whosoever therefore resisteth the power, resisteth the ordinance of God."

God put His authority, then, on human rulers in government. Good Christians must be subject to the authority of rulers.

Christians have a tendency to believe that, since all Christians are brothers and sisters in Christ, the distinctions between masters and servants have passed away. But that is not true. God commands, "Servants, be obedient to them that are your masters according to the flesh, with fear and trembling, in singleness of your heart, as unto Christ; not with eyeservice, as menpleasers; but as the servants of Christ, doing the will of God from the heart; with good will doing service, as to the Lord, and not to men" (Eph. 6:5-7).

Thus it is clear that in *authority* Christians are not all equal. Likewise in the same chapter, the Lord says, "Children, obey your parents in the Lord: for this is right. Honor thy father and mother; which is the first commandment with promise" (Eph. 6:1, 2).

Then in order to be a good Christian it is clear that a citizen must be subject to his rulers, a child subject to his parents, a servant subject to his master, a Christian subject to his pastor. God gives authority to some over others. Weak, frail humanity must have someone to rule over it.

And here let us note that the heart of all sin is rebellion against authority. By rebellion Satan fell from Heaven, angels followed him in the rebellion and are now shut up in darkness in chains awaiting judgment (II Peter 2:4). Rebellion is the heart of the crime and lawlessness which plagues America and other governments. Prodigal boys and wayward girls are simply rebellious against the authority of father and mother. And it is rebellion against Christ, a refusal to let Him reign, which is at the heart of all unbelief of Christ-rejecting sinners. The Saviour gave these words as picturing the heart-rebellion of those who do not love Him: "We will not have this man to reign over us" (Luke 19:14).

REBELLION AGAINST AUTHORITY IS THE SIN OF BOBBED HAIR, BOSSY WIVES, AND WOMEN PREACHERS

After introducing the subject of authority in Christian matters and commanding Christians to be followers of Paul as he followed Christ, the Holy Spirit gave the following verses in I Corinthians 11:3-9:

"*3 But I would have you know, that the head of every man is Christ; and the head of the woman is the man; and the head of Christ is God. 4 Every man praying or prophesying, having his head covered, dishonoureth his head. 5 But every woman that prayeth or prophesieth with her head uncovered dishonoureth her head: for that is even all one as if she were shaven. 6 For if the woman be not covered, let her also be shorn: but if it be a shame for a woman to be shorn or shaven, let her be covered. 7 For a man indeed ought not to cover his head, forasmuch as he is the image and glory of God: but the woman is the glory of the man. 8 For the man is not of the woman; but the woman of the man. 9 Neither was the man created for the woman; but the woman for the man.*"

Notice carefully the divine order of rule and submission, the order of authority as given in verse 3: "*The head of every man is Christ; and the head of the woman is the man; and the head of Christ is God.*" God is the head of Christ, Christ is the head of man, and man is the head of woman.

The teaching about bobbed hair was *not* based on the custom of the times as many suppose. Some tell us that in those days bobbed hair was a sign of idolatry. Others say that bobbed hair on women was the sign of a fallen woman, according to the customs of the time, and that Paul was simply giving temporary instructions to fit the local situation. But this verse shows plainly that could not be. Whatever bobbed hair meant then, it means now. Bobbed hair was forbidden then because of a deep-seated, fundamental, symbolical meaning. Long hair for a woman meant submission to her husband or father. Short hair meant rebellion against the God-given authority of father or husband. And the authority of the husband over the wife is as fundamentally settled as the authority of God over Christ and the authority of Christ over the man. *God first, then Christ, then man, then woman* is the divine order. The subject, then, involves much more than a woman's hair—it involves her heart. Bobbed hair is not so bad as bobbed character. The fashion of bobbed hair is forbidden because it is the symbol of the wicked fashion of rebellion of wives to their husbands' authority or of wicked daughters who rebel against their fathers. So we discuss the sin of bossy wives and women preachers before we discuss further the sin of bobbed hair.

And do not forget that most all girls intend or hope to be wives, and disobedient daughters are guilty of the same sin as bossy wives. Girls and unmarried women should have long hair for the same reason, as we will later show. But first let us find what God says about wives being subject to husbands and women subject to men.

CHAPTER III

WIVES TO SUBMIT THEMSELVES TO, BE SUBJECT TO, OBEDIENT TO THEIR HUSBANDS

We have just read in I Corinthians 11:3 that "the head of the woman is the man" and in verse 7 that man is "the image and glory of God; but the woman is the glory of the man," and in verse 9 that "neither was the man created for the woman; but the woman for the man." Here the Holy Spirit states a Bible doctrine, that there is and has been a fundamental difference in men and women ever since creation, because God made man to be the head of the woman.

Let us study some other Scriptures prayerfully that there may be no mistake about what God means here.

The first time this question of the authority of man over his wife comes up in the Bible is in Genesis 3 after we are told how sin brought ruin into the Garden of Eden. Before that, Genesis 2:18 plainly tells us that the woman was made after Adam and as a helpmeet for him. But as long as there was no sin, there was no need for laws. Adam and Eve perfectly loved each other, both agreed on every detail, and so there could never be any clash. But when sin came in, there were bound to be differences of opinion, and the rulership of man must be made plain.

In Genesis 3:16 the Scripture gives us the words of God unto Eve:

"Unto the woman he said, I will greatly multiply thy sorrow and thy conception; in sorrow thou shalt bring forth children; and thy desire shall be to thy husband, and he shall rule over thee."

Notice God's statement of the curse upon Eve and upon womankind: (1) woman was to have greatly increased sorrow and more frequent times of conception; (2) woman was to have pain or sorrow in childbirth; (3) woman must ask things she desired from her husband, and ask permission to do what she desired; (4) the husband was to rule over the wife.

"Thy desire shall be to thy husband, and he shall rule over thee!" How that would irk Dorothy Dix or Elsie Robinson, or other lady columnists, or feminists of the day! How shocked are they at the thought that a wife must sometimes ask her husband for money! How humiliating! So unspiritual women sometimes think! And yet that is exactly the position that God says that all womankind must take. Wives must make their desires known to their husbands and the husbands are to rule over their wives.

Some woman answers back, "Well, I'll never have any man bossing me around!" I know exactly how she feels. In fact I have felt the same way many a time. I would rather have my own way than to take orders. So would all the world. Every child sometimes feels the same way about his parents. Every pupil sometimes feels the same way about his teachers. Every citizen sometimes, I suppose, feels the same way about laws that he does not want to observe. It always did make me feel bad as I drove along the highway to hear behind me the scream of a highway police siren, and a harsh, brittle voice commanding me, "Pull over there and stop! Where is the fire? Didn't you see that sign that says, 'Speed limit 30 miles an hour'?" When I build a house, I would rather build it as I want to build it, instead of having to build it according to the city building code. And if I am going to live in America, I would rather be president, and since I live in Wheaton, Illinois, I would rather be mayor, and if I am to be a member of a church, I would rather be pastor. Of course there are complications that make that impossible, but what I mean is that every human spirit desires independence, does not want to be bossed, does not want any ruler. But we cannot have 131 million presidents, and every citizen in town cannot be mayor, and every person in a county cannot be sheriff! Not every member of a church can be pastor, not every workman can be general manager of the company, and not every member of the family can be head of the home. Yet God says there must be a head.

"Thy desire shall be to thy husband, and he shall rule over thee." Wives must be subject to the rule of their husbands if they fit into God's order of things. Does some wife who reads this find her heart rebellious against her husband? You do not want him to rule you? You do not want to obey? Then you feel just like all the criminals in the penitentiaries and jails feel. They, too, are rebels against God-given authority. They, too, want to be independent and have their own way. The very heart of the crime question is rebellion against authority. And most criminals were first allowed to get away with rebellion against the rule of parents in their own homes. Not being disciplined and controlled and conquered as children, they were not willing to be subject to the next authority God put over them, the authority of government. Criminals are simply rebels against authority and every rebellious wife has the same attitude of heart. You who read this do not want to have that attitude, and I trust you will carefully search your heart and ask God to take away any rebellion against His will or against those to whom He commands you to give obedience.

Even sinners who reject Christ do so primarily because they want their own way and are not willing to surrender their will to Him. Isaiah 53:6 says: "All we like sheep have gone astray; *we have turned every one to his own way.*" And Satan himself was once Lucifer, the son of the morning, evidently an archangel. He fell and became Satan by rebellion against God as you see from Isaiah 14:12-15. Rebellion against authority is the very heart of all sin.

Let us all, then, who love the Lord Jesus and seek to please Him earnestly try to overcome the rebellion of our natural human hearts and be subject to those whom God has put in authority over us, in government, in industry, in the school, in the church, and in the home. Wives, listen to the Word of God: "Thy desire shall be to thy husband, and he shall rule over thee."

The Bible is the Word of God, verbally inspired, and

therefore we find an exquisite accuracy in the way God deals with such questions. Notice that in the passage we have been discussing, Genesis 3:14-17, God speaks first to the serpent, and then to the woman and then to the man, Adam. God spoke first to the serpent because animals are to be subject to man, and mankind is to have dominion over all the beasts of the field. He spoke second to woman because she is to be subject to Adam, and God's rule for the woman is not conditioned at all on whether the man is what he ought to be.

Looking through the Bible we find this remarkable fact: when God is dealing with the whole family in their relation to God and their duty to God, He speaks to men first, but when He speaks to men and women *about their duty to each other,* then throughout the Bible He speaks first to the woman and then to the man.

"Every time God gives orders in the Bible to husbands and wives about their treatment of each other, He speaks to wives first, then to husbands. When He commands fathers and children about their duties to each other, He commands children first and then fathers. He commands servants first, then masters; subjects first, then rulers. God wants no excuses left to subjects who do not want to obey their rulers, a servant who does not want to obey his master, a child who does not want to obey his father, or a wife who does not want to obey her husband. When God speaks to people about their duties to Him, He speaks first to men. Where He speaks to people concerning their duties to others, He speaks first to wives, then to husbands. See how this works out in the passage beginning with Ephesians 5:22 and ending with Ephesians 6:9. See the same thing in the passage beginning in Colossians 3:18 and ending with Colossians 4:1, and likewise in I Timothy 6:1, 2.

"That rule is followed every place in the Bible where duties of wives and husbands to each other are discussed. Read carefully Genesis 3:16, 17, Ephesians 5:22-25, Colossians 3: 18, 19, and I Peter 3:1-7. God wants children to obey their parents even if the parents are wicked. Servants should obey their masters even if they are sometimes unkind. Citizens should obey the laws of their country even though they be administered by wicked and corrupt men. Likewise, God expects women to feel their duty to obey their husbands, good or bad, saved or unsaved. Nowhere in the Bible is a wife's duty to her husband conditioned on the kind of character he has or the way he treats her. This divine order in giving commands to men and women could not be an accident, but is evidently meant to leave those who should obey without any excuse for not doing so."*

We have given the command of Genesis 3:16 to women, "Thy desire shall be to thy husband, and he shall rule over thee." Now let us see other passages in the Bible, particularly in the New Testament, on this subject.

WIVES TO BE SUBJECT TO HUSBANDS "AS UNTO THE LORD" AND "IN EVERYTHING"

The book of Ephesians is full of rich and blessed teaching for the Spirit-filled Christian, one of the richest in the Bible. In Ephesians 5:22-24 is the following command:

"Wives, submit yourselves unto your own husbands, as unto the Lord. For the husband is the head of the wife, even as Christ is the head of the church: and he is the saviour of the body. Therefore as the church is subject unto Christ, so let the wives be to their own husbands in everything."

Then follows God's command to husbands, and the chapter ends with verse 33, which says:

"Nevertheless let every one of you in particular so love his wife even as himself; and the wife see that she reverence her husband."

Notice the plain command from God for Christian wives in this passage. First, wives are to *submit* themselves unto their own husbands (v. 22). Next, wives are to *be subject to* their husbands (v. 24). Last, wives are even to *reverence* their husbands (v. 33) or, as the Revised Version has it, *fear* them.

No passage in the Bible teaches so beautifully the marvelous intimacy and unity that the proper love and

---

* Quoted from the author's pamphlet, *Rebellious Wives and Slacker Husbands.*

Christian marriage brings to a husband and wife. They are indeed, as Jesus said, one flesh (Matt. 19:5; Genesis 2:24). Here we learn that the wife is to submit herself unto her husband as if he were Christ, literally "as unto the Lord." And verse 23 tells us: "For the husband is the head of the wife, even as Christ is the head of the church: and he is the saviour of the body."

We know that Christ is the Saviour of the church, which is His mystical body. We who have trusted Christ as Saviour are members of His body (Eph. 1:22, 23; I Cor. 12:12, 27). Thus Christ is the Saviour of His body.

But here we learn that the husband and wife are like Christ and His church. The husband and the wife have become one body, and the husband is the head of his wife. And the Lord says here in verse 23, "And he is the saviour of the body." The husband is to be the protector, the provider for, the savior of his wife's body. No man ought ever to marry who does not intend to take this place of serious responsibility. Some good wives work and should work to help with expenses, no doubt, but God lays that principal responsibility on the husband and father. He is the head of the wife, the head of the home, and is responsible as protector and savior. In other words, a man takes the relation to his wife that Christ takes to His spiritual body.

And for this reason, wives are to submit themselves to their own husbands "as unto the Lord." And "as the church is subject unto Christ, so let the wives be to their own husbands in everything" (v. 24).

Here is most holy ground. Husbands and wives should here take off their shoes from off their feet. Here is such holy love, such intimate oneness, such Christlike responsibility on the part of the husband, and such loving, even reverent submission on the part of the wife, that it must make all of us ashamed of our shallow, irresponsible or rebellious home relationships.

And notice that verse 24 says "in everything." I didn't write that. I even tremble and hesitate to emphasize it. But it is in the Bible. The Holy Spirit put it there, and I ought to call attention to it. A wife is to be subject to her hus-

band as if he were Christ. That means wives are to be subject to their husbands "in everything," just as the church is
to be subject to Christ.

If men do not want to take this holy responsibility, as
high priests in the home, then they ought not to marry. If
women do not want to take this meek and submissive attitude toward their husbands, then they sin against God,
against their husbands, and against their own future happiness when they marry. This is God's plan for a happy
home. God's plan works.

How many Christian women have learned that the way
to the greatest freedom and joy in the home is found in surrendering to obey the husband in everything! Mrs. Goforth, wife of the famous Canadian Presbyterian missionary
to China, Jonathan Goforth, tell us how this Scripture convicted her and led her to obedience to her husband. However, note that Mrs. Goforth agreed to obey her husband
"in all but matters of conscience," while the Bible commands wives to obey their husbands "in everything," men-
tioning no exceptions. But Mrs. Goforth's story is given for
the sweet testimony it bears that God's way of obedience
is the happy way for every wife. Mrs. Goforth says:

"Our children were all away at school. We were together
carrying on aggressive evangelism at a distant out-station.
The room given to us was dark and damp, with the usual
mud floor. The weather had turned cold, and there was no
place where one could get warm. I caught a cold. It was
not a severe one, but enough to make me rather miserable.
The third or fourth day, when the meetings were in full
swing and my organ was taking an attracting part, I became
possessed by a great longing to visit my dearly loved friend,
Miss H., living at the Weihuifu Station, some hours' run
south on the railway. But when I told my husband what I
had in mind, he strongly objected and urged against my going. I would not listen, even when he said my going would
break up at least the women's work. But I was determined
to go and ordered the cart for the trip to the railway. As
the cart started and I saw my husband's sad, disappointed,

white face, I would have stopped, but I wanted to show him I must have my way *sometimes!*

"Oh, what a miserable time I had till my friend's home in Weihuifu was reached! Miss H. gave one glance at my face and exclaimed: 'Whatever is the matter, Mrs. Goforth! Are you ill?'

"My only answer was to break down sobbing. Of course I could not tell her WHY. Miss H. insisted on putting me to bed, saying I was ill! She made me promise to remain there until after breakfast.

"The following morning, while waiting for breakfast, I opened my Testament and started to memorize, as usual, my three verses. Now it happened I was at that time memorizing the Epistle to the Ephesians and had reached the fifth chapter down to the twenty-first verse. The twenty-second, the first of the three to be memorized that morning, read: *'Wives, submit yourselves unto your own husbands as unto the Lord.'* I was, to say the least, startled! Somehow I managed to get this bravely memorized. Then going on to the twenty-third verse, these words faced me: 'For the husband is the head of the wife even as Christ is the head of the church: and he is the saviour of the body.'

"For a moment a feeling of resentment, even anger, arose. I could not treat this word as a woman once did, putting it aside with the remark: 'That is where Paul and I differ.' I believed the Epistle to the Ephesians was inspired, if any portion of Scripture was. How could I dare cut out this one part to which I was unwilling to submit? How I managed to memorize that twenty-third verse I do not know, for all the while a desperate mental struggle was on. Then came the twenty-fourth verse: 'Therefore as the church is subject unto Christ, so let the wives be to their own husbands in everything.'

"I could not memorize further: my mind was too agitated. 'It just comes to this,' I thought, 'Am I willing for Christ's sake to submit my will (in all but matters of conscience) to my husband?' The struggle was short but intense. At last I cried, *'For Christ's sake, I yield!'* Throwing a dressing gown about me, I ran to the top of the stairs and called to my friend, 'When does the next train go?'

" 'In about half an hour,' she replied, 'but you couldn't catch it and have your breakfast.'

" 'Never mind; I'm going to get that train!'

"My friend insisted on accompanying me to the station; we ate as we almost ran. With what joy I at last found myself traveling northward!

"On reaching my destination, imagine my surprise to find my husband, with a happy twinkle in his eye, standing on the platform!

" 'Why, Jonathan,' I cried, 'how did you know I was coming?'

"His reply was simply a happy, 'Oh, I knew you would come.'

"Later I told my husband frankly all I had passed through. What was the result? From that time, he gave me my way as never before, for does not verse twenty-five of the chapter quoted go on to say: 'Husbands, love your wives, even as Christ also loved the church, and gave himself for it.' A new realization of the need of *yieldedness* came to us both, which brought blessed results in our home life."*

WIVES TO BE SUBJECT TO HUSBANDS EVEN IN MATTERS OF CHRISTIAN WORSHIP AND SERVICE

In Ephesians 5:24, the wife is commanded: "Therefore as the church is subject unto Christ, so let the wives be to their own husbands in EVERY THING." For a wife to be subject in *everything* would mean she must be subject to him in matters of Christian worship and duty, and that is exactly what the Bible says. A husband and wife are one flesh. Being a Christian does not release a wife or a husband from this bond, which is to last until death. In matters of duty, even to God, the wife is to be subject to her husband. That sounds shocking, but let us consider a number of Scriptures on this question.

The first is I Corinthians 14:34, 35, which says: "Let

---

* Reprinted from *Climbing* by Mrs. Rosalind Goforth, by special arrangement with the Zondervan Publishing House, Grand Rapids, Michigan.

your women keep silence in the churches: for it is not permitted unto them to speak; but they are commanded to be under obedience, as also saith the law. And if they will learn anything, let them ask their husbands at home: for it is a shame for women to speak in the church."

We are not now discussing whether a woman should preach, and we must refer to this Scripture again when on that subject. But here, notice that in the church a woman is to be under obedience, "as also saith the law." What law? The law of Moses given in the first five books of the Bible. "The law" is a term very widely used in the New Testament, in reference to the books of Moses. The Scripture referred to is evidently Genesis 3:16 where to the woman it is said: "Thy desire shall be to thy husband, and he shall rule over thee." Thus we are told that that command, given to the first woman, holds good on down through the ages, even in New Testament times, and it includes even matters of worship. A Christian woman even in church is to be under obedience to her husband. And if she wants to know anything she is not to interrupt the services, but to wait until she gets home and there ask her own husband. Some wives do not like to ask their husbands; they had much rather talk to the preacher about it. And some husbands do not want to take this responsibility of leading the home in worship and in duty to God, but nevertheless this is God's plain command.

The woman, even in the church, is to be "under obedience, as also saith the law," we are told. Turning again to the law of Moses, in Numbers, chapter 30, we find further explanation of the position of wife and husband, daughter and father, in matters of duty to God. Read that chapter carefully and you will see that a young woman at home in her father's house could only make a vow to God subject to her father's approval. If the father "disallowed" the vow, it did not stand, and God would forgive her. If her father allowed it, and did not protest, the vow was allowed to stand as a binding obligation upon the woman. And likewise a wife, in the home of her husband, could make a vow to God only

subject to the approval of her husband. If her husband
"disallowed" it, the vow did not stand. She was not to fulfill it. But if her husband allowed it to stand, then the woman bound her soul by the vow and was held accountable to
keep it. Note that the husband or father must take the responsibility to God for a religious vow by the wife or daughter.

Numbers 30:10-13 reads as follows:

*"And if she vowed in her husband's house, or bound her
soul by a bond with an oath; And her husband heard it, and
held his peace at her, and disallowed her not: then all her
vows shall stand, and every bond wherewith she bound her
soul shall stand. But if her husband hath utterly made them
void on the day he heard them; then whatsoever proceeded
out of her lips concerning her vows, or concerning the bond
of her soul, shall not stand: her husband hath made them
void; and the Lord shall forgive her. Every vow, and every
binding oath to afflict the soul, her husband may establish it,
or her husband may make it void."*

It is clear from this that if a woman submits to her husband in these matters, God holds the husband accountable.
"He shall bear her iniquity" (v. 15). If the woman did
wrong in the matter, the husband is to blame.

This is a heavy responsibility upon a father and husband.
God has a high place of duty and authority for the man who
is the head of a home. God give us men to take that position, and women who respect it, and take the position God
has assigned to them! Even in matters of duty to God, a
wife is to be subject to her husband. So says the law. And
then we are told in I Corinthians 14:34, 35 that the same
rule applies to women in the New Testament. A woman,
even in church matters, is to be "under obedience, as also
saith the law."

Many a Christian wife is convinced that tithing is right.
She feels that she must tithe her husband's income, though
the husband is not convinced, or is not willing. What should
such a woman do? Should she slip out money without her
husband's knowledge or consent, and give it to the Lord's

work? Certainly not! To do so would be rebellion against her husband and disobedience to God. A wife may talk to her husband and take counsel with him, pleading with him to do what is right. But if she is to please God, she must submit herself to her husband in this matter as in other matters. And if the husband does wrong in not permitting his wife to tithe, "then he shall bear her iniquity," the Scripture says.

Many a wife has, in deliberate rebellion against her husband's orders, left her home to attend Christian services. She thought she was pleasing God, no doubt. Her Christian heart grew hungry for the fellowship of the saints and to hear the preaching of the Word of God. But she was not a better Christian by being a disobedient wife. She did not win her husband in that way. No, rather let the wife be so wholeheartedly subject to the husband, trusting God to help her win her husband, that the gospel will never be in reproach or blasphemed because of disobedient and rebellious wives. In the long run, any wife or daughter will get more freedom to worship God and serve Him with time and money by doing what God said in patient, trusting submission to her husband or father.

You remember that Joshua said, "But as for me and my house, we will serve the Lord" (Joshua 24:15). In the matter of duty to God and divine worship, Joshua assumed the responsibility for his entire household, his wife and children and servants! Even in matters of worship and service to God, the man is the head of his home, and the wife is to be subject to her husband.

God said of Abraham, "For I know him, that he will command his children and his household after him, and they shall keep the way of the Lord . . ." (Gen. 18:19). In matters of religion and duty to God, Abraham *commanded* "his children and his household." Abraham assumed that God-given authority and exercised it; Sarah and Isaac and the servants submitted to that authority. If you read Genesis, chapter 22, the account of the offering of Isaac, you will be greatly impressed to note that not once did Abraham ask

Sarah if she were willing for Isaac to be offered, nor did he even ask Isaac if he were willing to die! Rather Abraham took the sole responsibility to carry out God's plain orders.

Here is God's blessed way, that wives should be subject to their husbands and children to their parents, even in matters of worship and service to God.

In my boyhood home our dear father, now in Heaven, simply controlled the situation, and we went to church because our father saw that we went. It never entered the minds of any of us eight children to question whether we were going to church or not. Our father had already decided that for us! And in that authority our father followed the plain command of God. And that authority which a man exercises as head of his household extends to his wife even the same as to his children.

I recall that once in Dallas, Texas, I received a money order for $6.00 from a woman in Oklahoma. She asked that the money be applied on the radio broadcast expense and said, "Please do not acknowledge this gift over the radio nor by letter. I will be sure that you have received it anyway. If you should write a letter or announce it over the radio my husband might learn of my gift. He told me never to send any money to radio preachers. I took this money from that which he gave me for household expenses. I want the Lord to have it for the radio broadcast which has blessed so many people."

I wrote the lady that I could not receive the gift and returned her money order, telling her why. She wrote me again and said, "I gave fifty dollars this way on our new church building, taking the money out a little at a time from that which my husband gave me for the expense of the household. Other preachers have taken money given in this way without any protest." But I replied that however much the money would be appreciated as a gift for the Lord's work under other circumstances, I could not be a party to her disobedience to her husband in this matter. God is not pleased with rebellion, even though it be, ostensibly, because of love for Him. God wanted a meek and quiet spirit in the heart of that Christian woman, wanted her to be subject to her husband, more than he wanted $6.00 for a gospel radio program.

AGED WOMEN SHOULD TEACH YOUNG WOMEN TO OBEY HUSBANDS

Titus, the younger pastor, was instructed by Paul how to teach sound doctrine. In Titus 2:3-5 the Holy Spirit had Paul to write down the following:

"The aged women likewise, that they be in behaviour as becometh holiness, not false accusers, not given to much wine, teachers of good things;That they may teach the young women to be sober, to love their husbands, to love their children,To be discreet, chaste, keepers at home, good, obedient to their own husbands, that the word of God be not blasphemed."

Older women sometimes are responsible for breaking homes. When trouble comes up in the home of a young married couple, the mother of the wife may say, "You don't have to put up with his mistreatment! Get your things together and come back home if he doesn't treat you right! Stand up for your rights!" And the neighbor women take it on themselves to offer advice. But here we are told just the kind of counsel that the aged women should give to young women. They are to "teach the young women . . . to be discreet, chaste, keepers at home, good, OBEDIENT TO THEIR OWN HUSBANDS, that the word of God be not blasphemed." When a Christian woman's influence leads another woman to be rebellious and disobedient at home in her attitude toward her husband, then she sins against God and causes the Word of God to be blasphemed. Any kind of Christianity that does not make a woman into a good wife brings reproach on the cause of Christ. So older women must teach young wives to obey their husbands, and thus Christianity will be in repute, and God will be honored by the happy homes that Christianity brings!

Once I was asked to marry a young couple whom I loved

very dearly. The young bride-to-be asked me, "You are not going to put *obey* in the marriage ceremony, are you?" I answered back that of course I would not want to make up my own kind of marriage ceremony. "But," I said, "if I leave it out, God has put it in. It is in the Bible that wives are to be 'obedient to their own husbands.' You don't want me to leave out what God put in, do you?" And since she was a good Christian girl, she agreed. Preachers, to please a modern world, may leave *obey* out of the marriage ceremony. But God puts it in just the same and preachers ought to too, and no Christian wife pleases Him who does not take the solemn vow to obey her husband and who does not prayerfully, with God's help, seek to fulfill that vow.

CHRISTIAN WIVES TO BE IN SUBJECTION EVEN TO UNSAVED HUSBANDS

A question which often comes to intelligent and earnest Christian women on this matter is this: Supposing that her husband is unsaved, that his ideals are entirely different from Christian ideals, and that he does not obey the Bible commands, should a Christian wife obey such a husband?

How wonderfully adequate the Bible is! God answers this very question exquisitely. In I Peter, the third chapter, verses 1 and 2, we read:

"Likewise, ye wives, be in subjection to your own husbands; that, if any obey not the word, they also may without the word be won by the conversation of the wives; while they behold your chaste conversation coupled with fear."

In Titus 2:5 we learned that the Word of God would not be blasphemed if Christianity makes wives obedient to their own husbands. And here we learn that even unsaved husbands will be "won by the conversation of the wives" though they will not listen to the Bible, and will not obey the Word of God for themselves, otherwise.

Many a woman has wept and prayed many, many years, hoping that her husband would be saved. Yet rebellion in her heart against her husband and against God's authority through her husband has blocked the answer to her prayers! The way for a woman to win her unsaved husband is to be subject to him. If being a Christian doesn't make a woman into a good wife, then that is a poor recommendation of Christianity to the unsaved husband. No woman can be a good Christian who is not a good wife.

After all, the very heart of sin is rebellion against authority. And many a husband, seeing what gentleness, what submission, what transformed heart and life has resulted from his wife's trusting Christ as her Saviour, has hungered after the same Saviour and found the same peace of heart! The way to win unsaved husbands who will not listen to the Bible is for their wives to be subject to them.

This passage above, I Peter 3:1, 2, is followed in verses 3 to 7 by the plain teaching that men cannot be won, either to the Lord or to the wives permanently, by such outward adorning as the plaiting of the hair, the wearing of gold and the putting on of apparel. Read them carefully.

"Whose adorning let it not be that outward adorning of plaiting the hair, and of wearing of gold, or of putting on of apparel; But let it be the hidden man of the heart, in that which is not corruptible, even the ornament of a meek and quiet spirit, which is in the sight of God of great price. For after this manner in the old time the holy women also, who trusted in God, adorned themselves, being in subjection unto their own husbands: Even as Sara obeyed Abraham, calling him lord: whose daughters ye are, as long as ye do well, and are not afraid with any amazement. Likewise, ye husbands, dwell with them according to knowledge, giving honour unto the wife, as unto the weaker vessel, and as being heirs together of the grace of life; that your prayers be not hindered" (1 Peter 3:3-7).

The Bible does not forbid a woman putting on apparel (clothes), of course, but it forbids a woman looking upon her clothes as her real adornment, as her real beauty, as her real influence. No, the wifely beauty which women should seek is that of a meek and quiet spirit which is in the sight of God of great price. Sarah had it, verse 6 tells us, and

"obeyed Abraham, calling him lord." And the same marvelous influence that Sarah had over Abraham, godly wom-
en today have over their husbands if they honestly love
them, reverence them, *and obey them!* That is God's way to
win unsaved husbands!

The Bible has many paradoxes. Whosoever will save his
life shall lose it, Jesus said (Matthew 16:25). And the one
who really loses his life for Jesus' sake will find it. One
who exalts himself is to be abased, while one who humbles
self is to be exalted (Luke 18:14). The way up is down!
And so the way for a Christian woman to win her unsaved
husband both to herself and to God is to be submissive to
him, with such a meek and quiet spirit as will prove that
being a Christian really means a changed life and a surrender to the will of God and to those whom God has put in
authority over her.

Finally, to both the wife and the husband, the Holy
Spirit says that this divine order of wives being subject to
husbands and husbands loving their wives and giving honor
to them as the weaker vessel is to be followed in order "that
your prayers be not hindered." Many wives pray sincerely
and earnestly for their husbands to be saved. Their prayers
are hindered by their own rebellion! Husbands, too, find
their prayers hindered because they do not take the position
God wants them to take in the home as the stronger vessel,
as the head of the home, with loving benevolence, ruling as
a high priest, leading the home for God.

Will Not Unsaved Husbands Command Wives to Sin?

I have heard many objections at this point, and no doubt
many very earnest and sincere people will expect disaster to
come, if a Christian wife sets out to be subject to her unsaved husband. "Why, suppose my husband should command me to get drunk!" says a wife. "Don't you see that
would drag the wife down in sin with the unsaved husband?" says another. And many imaginary cases have been
presented to me by those who did not want to accept this
command of the Lord that wives are to be subject to their

husbands, even to unsaved husbands who do not obey the Word of God.

But to all such, I must simply answer that it is God's Word, and it is up to God to make it work. The Bible really works. God's way is better than all the smart ways that all the people of the ages have been able to invent. Wives can depend upon it that when God said this is the way to win an unsaved husband it is better than all the other ways she can devise.

But why should people suppose imaginary cases, contrary to the Word of God? Why should people believe that if a woman, obeying this command and believing this promise of God and setting out to win her husband, submitting to him with the whole heart as God commands—why should we believe that God would leave such a woman alone to break her heart, and to be led into sin as well as failure? I am sure that will never be the case with any woman who honestly and with all her heart and to please Jesus Christ, depending upon His Word, sets out to do just exactly what He says.

The plain, simple fact is that when a lost man sees his wife transformed before him, when he sees that she loves him in a new way, that she is quicker to please him than ever before, when he sees that because of her love for Christ she makes a more considerate wife, is more anxious to make him happy, and is easier to live with, such a man then is going to be glad of the great improvement in his wife. And however wicked he is, he will not want that beautiful and holy character desecrated and spoiled.

Not long ago a woman with flashing eyes tossed her head and said to me,

"Well, I'll certainly never obey my husband in everything. He is not a Christian; he goes to the tavern and he would even have me to go with him. But I'm for the Lord, and I'm against all his sin, and I tell him so. And I'm not going to obey him, either!"

Very kindly I said, "Well, aren't there other matters that

you differ on, too? Are there not other matters in which you refuse to obey your husband, matters where the Lord and Christianity and your Christian duty are not involved at all?"

"Yes," she replied, "we have regular cat-and-dog fights sometimes. I want my way about lots of things."

And then I told her that if she would first begin in all the matters where her rebellion had been only of her own stubborn will and not for Christ's sake, and in all these matters submit herself wholly to her husband's will, loving him, obeying him from the heart, seeking to please him, that then she could be sure that God would take her part and that she would never be led into sin on the other matters.

To every woman who reads this I would say if your husband's standards are lower than yours, and if he would lead you into sin, then begin first to surrender your own will in the matter of obedience, being surrendered to do whatever God commands. Make sure you do what God says, submitting to your husband in every detail which is not a matter of conscience. And then on the matter where you fear your husband would lead you into sin or command you to do wrong, you will find in him such a respect and such a gentleness as you never had believed possible in him.

Some woman says, "My husband wanted me to go to the tavern with him and drink beer." Another says, "My husband wants me to attend the picture show with him." No doubt that is true. Since you are the kind of Christian you are, your husband sees no reason why you should not drink beer or attend the picture show. But if you were the kind of Christian wife that God has pictured in His Word, so surrendered to the will of God that the rebellion is taken out of your heart, and that you have become, because you are a Christian, the kind of wife that every husband wants, submissive and loving and faithful and holy and good—if you were that kind of a wife, being subject to your husband as unto the Lord, your husband would not want to desecrate and defile and lead into sin such a lovely Christian character.

But note that to be subject to your husband, even an unsaved husband, does not mean to love what he loves, nor to give way to sin. Though I must keep the laws of the land and abide by traffic rules, to be a good citizen as I must to be a good Christian, I do not need to adopt the moral standards of any wicked traffic cop. A Christian boy should honor his father and obey his father, even though the father be an unconverted drunkard. But the boy should not start out to be a drunkard. And so a wife may be subject to her husband, as the Bible requires, and yet be sold out wholly for Jesus Christ. The Bible is not teaching here that a Christian woman should let down her standards of living to be like an unconverted husband. Rather the Scripture is saying that the Christian wife should attain to such a height of wifely surrender and Christian love that she may win her husband to Christ. Let no woman take this article or the Scriptures here quoted as permission to go into sin because the husband sinned. That is not the sense of the Scriptures. But rather, God is teaching Christian women to quit their sinful rebellion and self-will and submit to His authority in the husband as well as elsewhere.

After all, it is not up to me to make His plan work. That is up to God. It is His command and His promise, not mine. But I would stake all I am and have on the blessed truth that you can count on God's way working just as He says it will. "Wives, be in subjection to your own husbands; that, if any obey not the word, they also may without the word be won by the conversation of the wives; While they behold your chaste conversation coupled with fear."

WHAT IF WIVES ARE WISER THAN HUSBANDS?

Wives sometimes say, "But I have a better education than my husband. I am a better manager. I have better judgment in many matters. Why shouldn't I have the deciding voice? I think the wiser of the two should have the authority in the home."

Well, no doubt children often think they are wiser than their parents. Laborers are generally wiser, in their own sight, than their bosses. And no doubt the devil thinks himself wiser than God. That does not prove it is true.

However, children are often better informed, better trained, better equipped, in some matters, than their parents. Many a farm boy under the supervision of his county agent has learned to grow more corn to the acre than his father could, has learned to grow prize winning pigs by a feeding schedule with which his father is unfamiliar. But the farm boy still should not boss his father.

A girl in high school may learn how to make curtains, how to make lovely dresses, how to set an exquisite table, how to plan a balanced meal better than her mother ever knew. But God's plan is still for the girl to be subject to her mother.

I may be a better man than the policeman at the corner who directs traffic, and yet if I am a good citizen, I obey his whistle. I may be a better man than the judge, but I respect the court.

God's way is still the best way, and wives are to be subject to their husbands. It is the way of peace and happiness and prosperity.

I have no doubt that many of the curses on our land come from sin in the home. Children do not obey parents, because there is disunion and no respect for authority in the home. The crime wave that plagues America is a part and parcel of the rebellion against authority in which every woman who does not obey her husband has a part. Wives who do not submit to their husbands may expect their own children to scorn their authority. And such women need not be surprised if their husbands' love grows cold and all the horrible train of evil comes that follows rebellion against authority—quarrels, discontent, lack of trust, and then broken homes and broken hearts! And when such women come to pray, they may expect to be treated by the dear Lord as rebels, not only against the authority of husband, but against the authority of God who commanded wives to be subject to their own husbands as unto the Lord.

I had a letter the other day from a brokenhearted wife.

She had tried many, many years to win her husband to Christ. He would not hear her. She had heard me preach over the radio at Grand Island, Nebraska. She had found how she had failed in her rebellious way, trying to have her own way. And now she said, "I have tried my way and I have failed. Now I am going to try the Lord's way. It is my last chance to win my husband." Why don't you try God's way, dear wife who reads this?

In Oklahoma City by a book table in revival services, a woman pointed to my little booklet, *What Must I Do to Be Saved?* and said, "That booklet won my brother to Christ!" A man who stood nearby heard it. He pointed to the little booklet on *Rebellious Wives and Slacker Husbands* and said, "My brother and his wife were separated, had been separated two weeks, and were applying for a divorce. I got this little booklet for them and both of them read it. They went back together, confessed their sins to each other, and now their home is wonderfully happy."

Some years ago a woman wrote me in greatest distress. Her husband, she said, was so mean to her that it was impossible to live with him. She was having to give up her home and go back to her mother's. Yet her heart was broken about it and she wanted me to pray and wondered if there was anything she could do. I did pray and wrote to give her the Scriptures that I have given in these chapters about women being in subjection to their own husbands, and I sent her a little booklet on the subject. Soon she wrote to tell me that her home had been happily re-established. "I was as much to blame as he was," she said. "I was rebellious and bitter and wanted my own way. Now everything has been smoothed out and I love him as never before. Our hearts are, oh, so happy!"

Dear reader, God's way is the only way to bring real happiness in your home, permanent happiness. It is not much to do for one who loves the Lord, to be subject to your husband for Christ's sake. And oh, how rich are the rewards for any godly woman who obeys God through surrendering to the authority of her husband.

CHAPTER IV

WOMEN PREACHERS FORBIDDEN IN BIBLE

Should women preach? Does God call women to be pastors? Evangelists? Song leaders? Bible teachers for mixed classes of men and women?

If we try to settle this question by the opinion of men, it would never be satisfactorily settled. The great preponderance of opinion among responsible Christian people is indicated by the fact that most churches never call a woman preacher as pastor. Most seminaries never employ a woman teacher of theology. And relatively very few women find positions of any sort on the faculties of seminaries and Bible institutes. Most churches have men to conduct evangelistic meetings, if they have such meetings. So the majority opinion would decide for men preachers and against women preachers. But opinions would vary with the preferences. The followers of Aimee Semple McPherson, the large Pentecostal and Holiness groups, the Volunteers of America who have been led so long by Maud Ballington Booth, The Salvation Army where women preachers have always been welcomed, though in actual practice they usually did not have the leadership—all these and many others would insist on the right of women to preach, to do the work of an evangelist or pastor, or Bible teacher, the same as a man of like attainments.

The matter cannot be settled by opinion. It cannot be settled by observation. It cannot be settled by logic. There is only one place to settle this question of whether God wants a woman to preach or not. That is *by the Word of God itself!* The Bible is the place to find what God wants people to do. The Bible is to tell us how the Lord's work is to be conducted. There is no other authority of the slightest value in this matter, except as it derives from the Bible, and coincides with the Bible teaching.

Women sometimes say that they feel *called* to preach. They say sometimes that the Holy Spirit has told them plainly they should preach. But we must remember that every false doctrine in the world is supported by the same argument. A mother who killed her afflicted child said that God told her to do it. Some people feel led of the Spirit of God to preach salvation by grace. Others say they feel led of the same Spirit of God to preach salvation by works! Some people feel led of God, they say, to be sprinkled for baptism, and others feel led of the same Spirit to be immersed for baptism. Some people feel led of God to persecute the Jews. Some people feel led of God to start unscriptural cults with false doctrines; that is, they honestly believe themselves so led. But the answer to all this is very simple. The Holy Spirit of God dictated the Bible. Holy men of God spoke as they were moved by the Holy Ghost. The Holy Spirit will never contradict His own Word. Any leading that is thought to be of the Holy Spirit should be checked by the Bible. Any leading that does not coincide with the plain teaching of the Word of God is false, and is not from God's Spirit. For this reason the Scripture commands us, "Beloved, believe not every spirit, but try the spirits whether they are of God: because many false prophets are gone out into the world" (I John 4:1).

This matter, then, cannot be settled by how people feel led except as it coincides with the Bible. No leading is from God if it goes against the plain statements of God's Word. This matter must be settled by the Bible, the supreme rule of faith and practice for Christians.

Let us very carefully consider the Scriptures that bear on this matter. The Bible is the Word of God; no passage of Scripture will contradict any other passage. And since man and woman and God have not changed, we will find that what God intended women to do in Bible times He intends them to do now, also. Let every reader with prayerful heart ask the Holy Spirit for wisdom, and then search out in the Scriptures you are given what God has to say about women preaching the gospel.

I TIMOTHY 2:11-15 SAYS NO WOMAN TO TEACH
OR USURP AUTHORITY OVER MEN

The first Scripture to which I call your attention on this matter of women preachers is in I Timothy 2:11-15, which is quoted here:

"11 Let the woman learn in silence with all subjection. 12 But I suffer not a woman to teach, nor to usurp authority over the man, but to be in silence. 13 For Adam was first formed, then Eve. 14 And Adam was not deceived, but the woman being deceived was in the transgression. 15 Notwithstanding she shall be saved in childbearing, if they continue in faith and charity and holiness with sobriety."

I want you to notice the universal character of this Scripture. It is in the letter written by Paul, the apostle to the Gentiles, addressed to Timothy. Paul had left Timothy at Ephesus to have oversight of the great work in that city, with many elders, as you will see in the first chapter of this book. Verse 3 shows that Timothy was to keep any from teaching false doctrines. Verse 4 shows that he was to keep down confusion, and verses 6 and 7 show that he was to set right some who desired "to be teachers of the law; understanding neither what they say, nor whereof they affirm." It is important to notice in this epistle, the first to Timothy, that we have detailed instruction about the qualifications for a bishop (or pastor) and of a deacon (see chapter 3). No one can read I Timothy without seeing that it sets forth rules and instructions for all New Testament churches, as delivered to Paul, the apostle to the Gentiles, by the Holy Spirit. So the passage we have read above is for all New Testament churches and New Testament Christians. To New Testament Christians Paul said, "Let the woman learn in silence with all subjection. But I suffer not a woman to teach, nor to usurp authority over the man, but to be in silence." Paul did not allow any women preachers or women teachers, nor any women to have authority over men, in any New Testament churches. Paul's word was accepted as law throughout the length and breadth of the Roman empire among fundamentally sound Christian people. At Rome, at Corinth, at Ephesus, the great centers, and all between Paul's authority as an apostle of God is recognized. And in no place, Paul says, would he allow a woman to teach or usurp authority over men.

And this rule of Paul is not arbitrary, but fits into the plan of God from the time of the creation. Paul explains that "Adam was first formed, then Eve. And Adam was not deceived, but the woman being deceived was in the transgression." God made Adam first. Eve was made second and as his helpmeet, subject to him. For that reason, says Paul, women are not to teach men in the church, are not to be chief officers in the church nor have authority over men. For women to take such authority is usurpation, unlawful seizing of an authority that is not properly and naturally theirs. From the creation, this Scripture says, women are to take the place of subjection, because they were not created to have authority over men or to teach men.

And again Paul says that the weakness of a woman and her aptness to be misled is shown because "Adam was not deceived, but the woman being deceived was in the transgression." Satan found he could deceive Eve easier than he could deceive Adam. God made a woman after such a fashion that she should be a comfortable and obedient helpmeet, a mate who would fit to his will and plans. So, in the nature of the case, women are not as well fitted for executive authority. If women are more easily led, they are not as good leaders. Every pastor knows that women are easier to enlist in good work. But careful observers must admit that women are also easier led into false doctrines and into errors of various kinds. But the argument here in I Timothy 2:14 is that Satan was able to deceive Eve when he could not deceive Adam, and that this is an evidence that women should not be placed in authority in churches and in Christian work. If he could deceive Eve easier in the Garden of Eden, he could deceive women easier now. This means that women leaders are more likely to lead into heresy in doctrine and unscriptural practice than men. Women are not fitted to teach men or usurp authority over men, says this Scripture. But also, in verse 15, God has a special duty and privilege for women in childbearing. If they submit themselves to God's plan in humility and meekness, then they shall be rescued and preserved, when pangs of childbirth are come upon them. Many godly women have found sweet comfort and ease and help in the time when they go down into the valley of the shadows to bring forth a child for the Lord, receiving help from God because they were willing to take a woman's place in submission.

Let us consider carefully verses 11 and 12.

1. The woman is to learn in silence, with all subjection.

2. A woman is not to teach. Certainly not to teach men, but evidently not to teach general groups, including men.

3. A woman is never to have authority over men.

4. And then again it is emphasized that a woman is to be "in silence" in such public services.

We know well that God does not want Christian women to remain silent outside the mixed public service. Titus 2:3, 4 plainly commands "the aged women likewise . . . That they may teach the young women." Here we are plainly told that old women may teach young women, and should do so. But they are to teach them, among other things, to be "obedient to their own husbands" (v. 5). Women are to be in silence, then, as far as teaching the whole church is concerned, or teaching men, or groups including men, but older women may teach younger women. It is clear that a mother may teach her own children, as Timothy's mother and grandmother evidently taught him (II Tim. 1:5). Proverbs 1:8 commands: "And forsake not the law of thy mother." Proverbs 6:20 says: "My son . . . forsake not the law of thy mother." Proverbs 30:17 says: "The eye that mocketh at his father, and despiseth to obey his mother, the ravens of the valley shall pick it out, and the young eagles shall eat it." A woman may teach other women and may teach children. But none of these cases we have mentioned refers to public teaching as an official of the church, or teaching of large mixed groups. Priscilla helped her husband, Aquila, to teach Apollos the way of the Lord more perfectly. But in this we may be sure that she had the meek spirit of a helpmeet to her husband. She spoke in private conversation, and not as an official teacher or as one having authority.

So when Paul said, "I suffer not a woman to teach, nor to usurp authority over the man, but to be in silence," it seems clear to me he is forbidding a woman to take a place as a public teacher of men. A woman is to be silent in the public assembly in the sense that she is not to teach as an official of the church. She particularly is to be silent as far as teaching men is concerned. That is plainly forbidden. No woman, according to this passage, is to be allowed to teach a class of men, or to teach a mixed class including men, nor to teach the church in a public assembly, including men.

It is equally clear that no woman is to take a place as an official of a church, having authority over men. No woman could be pastor of a church, according to this plain verse. To do so would be a usurpation of authority that was forbidden her.

In New Testament churches a woman's place was to be taught, not to teach. A woman's place was to be silent, not to be a public speaker. A woman's place was to be in subjection, and not to be in authority. Certainly this Scripture forbids any woman to be a preacher or pastor or evangelist.

It is fitting at this place, when God has forbidden a woman to take authority in religious matters, to remind you that pastors do have authority from God. Consider the third chapter of I Timothy, which follows this passage, and its discussion of the office of a bishop. The word *bishop* means overseer, and is a New Testament word for pastor. Certainly an overseer has authority. This authority is indicated also in I Timothy 3:5 which says: "For if a man know not how to rule his own house, how shall he take care of the church of God?" A man needs to know how to rule to be a bishop or overseer or pastor of a church. But a woman is plainly forbidden to rule, so a woman could not be a pastor according to the New Testament plan.

In Hebrews 13:17 we are commanded to "obey them that have the rule over you, and submit yourselves," and he speaks of spiritual rulers that watch over our souls, that is, pastors and Christian leaders. Again in Hebrews 13:24 the author says by inspiration of the Holy Spirit, "Salute all them that have the rule over you," manifestly referring to Christian leaders. Pastors and preachers have a real authority from God to rule. But a woman is not to have authority over men, and so a woman could not be a pastor of a church, or a preacher of the gospel, in the ordinary sense.

An evangelist also must speak with authority. Paul commanded Timothy, "Do the work of an evangelist" (II Tim. 4:5). But Timothy, the evangelist, was also given these instructions: "These things command and teach. Let no man despise thy youth . . ." (I Tim. 4:11, 12). An evangelist has authority from God and must not be despised, even though young. But no woman is to take authority over men, and no woman can be an evangelist in the Bible sense. There were no women evangelists in Bible times and there should be none now.

I CORINTHIANS 14:34, 35 COMMANDS WOMEN TO BE SILENT IN THE CHURCH

Once before we studied those two verses in the fourteenth chapter of First Corinthians which deal with the woman's place in the church. But we discussed only the teaching that women are, even in religious and church matters, subject to their husbands. Let us read verses 34 and 35 again, and see what they say about women preachers.

"Let your women keep silence in the churches: for it is not permitted unto them to speak; but they are commanded to be under obedience, as also saith the law. And if they will learn anything, let them ask their husbands at home: for it is a shame for women to speak in the church" (I Cor. 14:34, 35).

Again, the Scripture expressly commands that women are to keep silence in the churches, that it is not permitted unto them to speak, but they are to be under obedience, just as they were to be according to the Old Testament.

Someone may say that this rule was only for the church at Corinth. But that is not true. This epistle is not only written to the Christians at Corinth, but also to "all that in every place call upon the name of Jesus Christ our Lord, both their's and our's," as you see from the second verse of the first chapter. The instructions of I Corinthians were given by the Holy Spirit to all Christians everywhere. Then, to all Christians everywhere, the Lord commands: "Let your women keep silence in the churches: for it is not permitted unto them to speak; but they are commanded to be under obedience, as also saith the law," and "It is a shame for women to speak in the church."

Some may say that according to this Scripture a woman should not sing in the choir, should not testify in a prayer meeting. We will deal with that further on. I think that the Lord means a woman should be silent as far as official teaching or preaching is concerned, any public expounding of the Scriptures, or any public leadership of the church, or of men, or of groups containing men. If that interpretation does not go far enough, let us go just as far as the Scripture intends. But at least it is clearly and obviously true that this Scripture forbids any woman to preach, forbids any woman to take the place of a pastor or an evangelist. That was simply not permitted in any New Testament church, and it is not permitted now anywhere if people are to obey the plain command of God.

Again notice that in this matter of the relations of men and women, God's will has never changed. Women are to be in obedience in the churches in these days just as women were to be in obedience and silent in the Old Testament worship. In the Old Testament family, the wife was to be subject to her husband. In the Old Testament tabernacle and temple worship, there were no women priests, no women scribes, no women officials. And this passage says that the same thing is to be true of the women in the New Testament.

Reviewing again the two passages of Scripture which particularly forbid women preachers, note that in I Corinthians 14:34, 35, the woman is to be silent "in the church." But in I Timothy 2:11, 12 it is forbidden a woman to teach or to usurp authority over the men anywhere. *The church is not mentioned.* It is forbidden a woman to take an official part in a church service, yes. But it is equally forbidden a woman to teach men or usurp authority over men outside of the church service. It is as wrong for a woman to take the place of a Bible teacher or pastor or evangelist in a private home or in a Sunday school class as if it were in an official, so-called "church service." God simply did not intend for woman to have a place of authority or leadership over men or to teach men.

There Were No Women Pastors, Evangelists, Bible Teachers, or Preachers in the New Testament Times

We have considered the plain commands of the Bible forbidding women to preach. Now I call your attention to the fact that these commands were everywhere obeyed in New Testament churches. In not a single New Testament church was any woman allowed to be pastor or evangelist or Bible teacher. In not a single New Testament church was there a woman preacher. There were twelve original apostles, their names were given, but there was not a woman among them. Sermons are given in the New Testament, as preached by a number of preachers, but never a sermon is mentioned as having been preached by any woman.

All the words used for preachers in the Bible are masculine words. *Elder* is a masculine word. *Bishop* is a masculine word. Those mentioned as teachers in the New Testament were men. The masculine pronoun is used throughout the qualifications of a bishop in I Timothy 3:1-7. He must be the husband of one wife (only one). In that short passage referring to bishops or pastors, *he* is used five times; *his,* three times; *a man,* twice; *husband,* one time. The Bible makes no allowance for any bishop except those that are men. Check and count those words in the first seven verses of I Timothy 3.

Many godly women are mentioned in the New Testament. Let no one deceive you about the women of the New Testament. They were often as well trained, as devout, as well instructed as the men. Consider the faith (doctrine) of Lois and Eunice, the grandmother and mother of Timothy (II Timothy 1:5). Consider the remarkable spiritual insight given to Mary, the mother of Jesus, how she pondered the things in her heart, even before the birth of the Saviour. To her the angel had appeared, telling her wonderful facts about the coming Saviour (Luke 1:28-38). Mary was a spiritual girl, even filled with the Holy Spirit, as you see from her praises to God in the presence of Elizabeth, in Luke 1:46-55. Mary went with Jesus most of the time. What a wonderfully developed Christian she must have been! And yet Mary never preached, never taught men, never took any official position in any church.

Consider another Mary, the sister of Lazarus and of Martha. She sat at the feet of Jesus and heard His teaching, and so delighted in it that she would not give it up for preparing meals (Luke 10:38-42). Jesus was pleased. He commended her and taught her. Later Mary came to anoint Jesus with a pound of ointment of spikenard, very costly (John 12:1-7), and Jesus said, "Let her alone: against the day of my burying hath she kept this." Mary had saved her money, had carefully laid away this beautiful, expensive gift to anoint Jesus just before his death on the cross. She seemed to understand better than any of the apostles that Jesus was going to the cross. Judas complained that the money was not spent for the poor, and the other disciples seem to have felt just as Judas did (Matt. 26:8, 9). Jesus had great joy at the spiritual insight of this godly and spiritually wise woman, and promised that what she had done would be told throughout the world for a memorial to her. And yet Mary, no matter how wise and well taught she was, was never a preacher, never a pastor, never a Bible teacher!

A number of other prominent women were mentioned in

the New Testament. Phoebe, the servant or deaconess of the church at Cenchrea, was a very useful and godly woman (Romans 16: 1, 2). But she is never mentioned as a teacher or preacher or any official. She was gladly content to wait on the poor and do the work of a servant of the church, not a ruler or teacher or preacher.

Priscilla, the wife of Aquila, is mentioned several times in the New Testament, and she must have been a very devout Christian woman, but she is never mentioned as a preacher or teacher, pastor or evangelist.

There were no women preachers, no women pastors nor evangelists nor Bible teachers, in the New Testament churches.

WERE PROPHETESSES PREACHERS?

In the Bible several women were called prophetesses, including Miriam (Ex. 15:20), Deborah (Judges 4:4), Huldah (II Kings 22:14), Noadiah (Neh. 6:14), Anna (Luke 2:36), four daughters of Philip (Acts 21:9). Some people who never studied the matter think that prophetesses were preachers. But they were not. It is never mentioned that a single one of these prophetesses preached or addressed public congregations of people in any way. Prophetesses were not preachers. They did not preach; they did not do the work of a pastor nor the work of an evangelist, nor of a Bible teacher.

To prophesy means to speak by divine revelation. A prophecy is a special revelation by the Spirit of God. A prophet is a man who receives a divine revelation. A prophetess is a woman who receives divine revelation concerning the future.

Prophets (masculine) were sometimes also preachers. Isaiah, Jeremiah, Daniel and Ezekiel all preached. But they were primarily prophets, that is, they received divine revelation of what should happen to Israel. They were also preachers, though they are called prophets. But prophetesses never preached in the Bible. They received brief divine revelation to give to individuals, but were never sent to preach, to address public assemblies as expounders of the Word, nor to do the work of a pastor or evangelist.

The meaning of the words *prophet* and *prophetess* in the Old Testament is the same as the word *prophet* and *prophetess* in the New Testament.

The work of a prophet is indicated in Deuteronomy 18:22 which says:

"When a prophet speaketh in the name of the Lord, if the thing follow not, nor come to pass, that is the thing which the Lord hath not spoken, but the prophet hath spoken it presumptuously: thou shalt not be afraid of him."

The word of a prophet is supposed to come to pass, that is, *prophecy is usually a divine revelation of the future.*

In the New Testament, many, many times the Scripture indicates that the words of a prophet are a foretelling of the future. For instance, Matthew 1:22 says: "Now all this was done, that it might be fulfilled which was spoken of the Lord by the prophet." See also Matthew 2:17, Matthew 2:23, Matthew 3:3, Matthew 4:14, Matthew 12:17, Matthew 21:4, Matthew 26:56, Matthew 27:9, Matthew 27:35. I have mentioned only Scriptures in the Gospel of Matthew and there are many others in the New Testament, all which speak of the fulfilling of the words of some prophet of the Old Testament. I say a prophet usually foretells the future by divine revelation. A prophetess, likewise, is one who receives divine revelation.

The only book in the New Testament that God calls a prophecy is the book of Revelation. "The book of this prophecy" (Rev. 22:19) is Revelation, the New Testament book which is given over almost entirely to a revelation of future events. Prophecy does not mean preaching; it means a divine revelation under the anointing of the Spirit. A prophetess does not preach.

In the New Testament, Peter, John, and Paul are not called prophets (though God used each of them to write down some prophecies in His Word), but their primary work was preaching. On the other hand, Agabus is twice mentioned in the Book of Acts as a prophet. His first prophecy is mentioned in Acts 11:27, 28 which says:

"And in these days came prophets from Jerusalem unto Antioch. And there stood up one of them named Agabus, and signified by the Spirit that there should be great dearth throughout all the world: which came to pass in the days of Claudius Caesar."

Agabus very briefly gave a revelation God had given to him of a dearth that would come on the world.

Again, Acts 21:10, 11 tells about another prophecy of this man, Agabus, in the following words:

"And as we tarried there many days, there came down from Judœa a certain prophet, named Agabus. And when he was come unto us, he took Paul's girdle, and bound his own hands and feet, and said, Thus saith the Holy Ghost, So shall the Jews at Jerusalem bind the man that owneth this girdle, and shall deliver him into the hands of the Gentiles."

Note again this is a very simple message from God about what would happen to Paul at Jerusalem. It took less than a verse to record it. There was no sermon to it. The message was probably given to Paul and Luke and perhaps Timothy or other friends. It was not in any sense a sermon, just a simple revelation from God of what would occur. That is what prophesying is. And just before this prophet Agabus is mentioned in verse 10, the preceding verse (Acts 21:9) tells of Philip: "And the same man had four daughters, virgins, which did prophesy," that is, these virgin daughters received special revelations from God. They did not preach.

I Corinthians 14:1, 5 indicates that it would be blessed for all Christians to prophesy. It does not mean that every Christian is to be a preacher, a pastor, an evangelist. Rather, every Christian should be so close to God that God would reveal to him sometimes things that will happen in the future. Likewise, I Corinthians 14:24 does not mean that if every person in the congregation got up and preached a sermon that all the unbelievers present would be saved. It means that if there were clear evidence that every Christian was in such intimate touch with God as to receive a revelation from Him about what to do and what would happen, it would convince every gainsayer of the truth of the gospel. I Corinthians 14:39 indicates that every Christian should covet this close touch with God and that God would reveal His will to us and the things that we especially need to know about how to meet the future. And remember that that was much more needed before the New Testament was written than it is needed now, when we have the divine revelation of the Bible complete.

There are two misleading notes in the Scofield Bible on this question of prophecy. Concerning I Corinthians 12:10 Dr. Scofield comments, "The N. T. prophet is not ordinarily a foreteller, but rather a forth-teller, one whose gift enabled him to speak 'to edification, and exhortation, and comfort' (I Cor. 14:3)." But I Corinthians 14:3 does not say and does not mean that a New Testament prophet is any different from an Old Testament prophet. A divine revelation, a prophecy, from God does bring edification, exhortation, and comfort, as I Corinthians 14:3 says. But there is not one verse of Scripture that indicates that prophecy is preaching or that there is any difference in the offices of an Old Testament prophet and a New Testament prophet.

Again, commenting on I Corinthians 14:1 Dr. Scofield says, "The N. T. prophet was not merely a preacher, but an inspired preacher, through whom, until the N. T. was written, new revelations suited to the new dispensation were given (I Cor. 14:29, 30)." This statement is misleading. By preacher we mean one who expounds the Bible. But a prophecy was not expounding the Bible but was *an entirely new revelation from God.* Some unlearned people have seized on these notes as an excuse for women preachers. But prophecy is not preaching; it is an entirely new revelation from God, referring usually, as far as we know, to the future, and certainly being a direct, immediate revelation, not an exposition of Scripture, not Bible teaching nor evangelism nor preaching. Prophecy is not preaching. Prophetesses in the Bible never preached.

Acts 2:17, 18 gives us a blessed prophecy of the future. It is quoted from the prophet Joel and says,

"And it shall come to pass in the last days, saith God, I will pour out of my Spirit upon all flesh: and your sons and your daughters shall prophesy, and your young men shall see visions, and your old men shall dream dreams: And on my servants and on my handmaidens I will pour out in those days of my Spirit; and they shall prophesy."

There is coming a time when the Holy Spirit will be poured out upon all flesh so that both sons and daughters shall prophesy, and servants and handmaidens, too. But that prophesying does not mean that all will be preachers or evangelists or Bible teachers. It means that in the fulness of the Holy Spirit, every Christian then will be in touch with God; and God will reveal Himself, and things we ought to know, to every Christian, so Christians can warn one another.

Deborah, the prophetess in the Old Testament, did not preach and she took no authority over men. The story is told in Judges 4:4-9. Read it and you will see that it did not involve any authority over men and certainly did not involve preaching.

"4 And Deborah, a prophetess, the wife of Lapidoth, she judged Israel at that time. 5 And she dwelt under the palm tree of Deborah between Ramah and Bethel in mount Ephraim: and the children of Israel came up to her for judgment. 6 And she sent and called Barak the son of Abinoam out of Kedesh-naphtali, and said unto him, Hath not the Lord God of Israel commanded, saying, Go and draw toward mount Tabor, and take with thee ten thousand men of the children of Naphtali and of the children of Zebulun? 7 And I will draw unto thee to the river Kishon Sisera, the captain of Jabin's army, with his chariots and his multitude; and I will deliver him into thine hand. 8 And Barak said unto her, If thou wilt go with me, then I will go: but if thou

wilt not go with me, then I will not go. 9 And she said, I will surely go with thee: notwithstanding the journey that thou takest shall not be for thine honour; for the Lord shall sell Sisera into the hand of a woman. And Deborah arose, and went with Barak to Kedesh."

Deborah lived under a palm tree and "the children of Israel came up to her for judgment." There was no government in the land. When two neighbors had a dispute and could not come to an agreement, they said, "We will go and ask Deborah to decide." So they came to Deborah and she would advise, possibly by divine revelation, how to settle the difference. And those who wished would take her decision. She had no authority. Any good Christian can mediate between neighbors today.

That is exactly how New Testament Christians are counseled to settle their differences. I Corinthians 6:1-8 plainly says that Christians are not to go to law and have differences settled by authority, but they are commanded, "If then ye have judgments of things pertaining to this life, set them to judge who are least esteemed in the church," that is, one who is not called to be a preacher or any kind of officer or leader in the church is yet capable, by the Spirit of God, of knowing what to do when asked to mediate between Christians. Judging between others in that sense has nothing to do with law or authority. It simply means that Spirit-filled Christians can find the mind of God, and that is the way Deborah judged or acted as a mediator between people in a land when there was no king or ruler and when people voluntarily brought her a matter to ask her advice.

Note that the prophecy of Deborah given in Judges 4:6, 7 is a divine revelation. Note that it takes less than two verses to record it, and note that it was addressed to one man, Barak. In verse 9 God gave Deborah a further revelation in this phrase, "For the Lord shall sell Sisera into the hand of a woman," and shows that Barak's insistence on taking Deborah with him displeased the Lord. Deborah was not a preacher, not a leader. God did not want her leading the army. She did not take authority over men and did not teach men. She simply delivered a brief message from God to Barak.

Miriam, the sister of Moses and of Aaron, is called a prophetess in Exodus 15:20. There we are told that "Miriam the prophetess, the sister of Aaron, took a timbrel in her hand; and all the women went out after her with timbrels and with dances. And Miriam answered them, Sing ye to the Lord." Miriam led women in singing. She never led the men in singing nor preached to men.

But Miriam the prophetess was used of God as a startling object lesson to women who seek authority and leadership in religious matters, and God cursed her with leprosy for her sin. In Numbers 12:1-15, this remarkable story is told.

"And Miriam and Aaron spake against Moses because of the Ethiopian woman whom he had married: for he had married an Ethiopian woman. And they said, Hath the Lord indeed spoken only by Moses? hath he not spoken also by us? And the Lord heard it. (Now the man Moses was very meek, above all the men which were upon the face of the earth.) And the Lord spake suddenly unto Moses, and unto Aaron, and unto Miriam, Come out ye three unto the tabernacle of the congregation. And they three came out. And the Lord came down in the pillar of the cloud, and stood in the door of the tabernacle, and called Aaron and Miriam: and they both came forth. And he said, Hear now my words: If there be a prophet among you, I the Lord will make myself known unto him in a vision, and will speak unto him in a dream. My servant Moses is not so, who is faithful in all mine house. With him will I speak mouth to mouth, even apparently, and not in dark speeches; and the similitude of the Lord shall he behold: wherefore then were ye not afraid to speak against my servant Moses? And the anger of the Lord was kindled against them; and he departed. And the cloud departed from off the tabernacle; and, behold, Miriam became leprous, white as snow: and Aaron looked upon Miriam, and, behold, she was leprous. And Aaron said unto Moses, Alas, my lord, I beseech thee, lay not the sin upon us, wherein we have done foolishly, and wherein we have

*sinned. Let her not be as one dead, of whom the flesh is half
consumed when he cometh out of his mother's womb. And
Moses cried unto the Lord, saying, Heal her now, O God, I
beseech thee. And the Lord said unto Moses, If her father
had but spit in her face, should she not be ashamed seven
days? let her be shut out from the camp seven days, and
after that let her be received in again. And Miriam was
shut out from the camp seven days: and the people jour-
neyed not till Miriam was brought in again."*

Note from the above that Miriam and Aaron said, "Hath
the Lord indeed spoken only by Moses? hath he not spoken
also by us?" Miriam and Aaron were both in the same sin.
And in verse 9 the Scripture says, "And the anger of the
Lord was kindled against them." God was angry with Miriam and with Aaron because each of them wanted to usurp
authority. BUT MIRIAM ONLY WAS STRICKEN WITH
LEPROSY FOR HER SIN! The difference was that Aaron
had been appointed of God as the high priest. Aaron was a
man and was given a man's place. So Miriam's sin was much
more wicked than that of Aaron, and God made of her an
appalling object lesson to all women who would seek to take
authority or leadership over men or alongside men. Miriam
was a prophetess, but even a woman who is a prophetess sins
terribly against God when she seeks leadership as a preacher, teacher, evangelist or leader over men.

In Matthew 28:10 Jesus gave a divine revelation, a message to two women. He said, "Be not afraid: go tell my
brethren that they go into Galilee, and there shall they see
me." It is never wrong for a woman to run an errand for
the Lord. But that is not preaching. That is not doing the
work of a pastor or the work of an evangelist. That does
not authorize any woman to speak in public to a mixed congregation.

So the Bible fits in every part, in practice and teaching.
Paul said, "Let the woman learn in silence with all subjection. But I suffer not a woman to teach, nor to usurp authority over the man, but to be in silence" (I Tim. 2:11, 12).
It was in exact accordance with the teaching and practice of

all the Old Testament and all the New Testament. No
prophetess in the Bible violated this plain command. They
did not teach men nor teach the church and they did not
take any place of authority over men.

Even prophetesses obeyed the command of I Corinthians
14: 34, 35 to keep silence in the churches and be under obedience and if they would know anything, they asked their
husbands at home.

Arguments for Women Preachers Answered

It is noteworthy that very few people try to prove *from
the Bible* that women ought to preach. The Bible has no
command for women to preach. So when women want to
preach, they usually get their reasons outside the Bible and
bring arguments from human observation or reason. Let us
notice some of these arguments.

(1) "Women preachers have done so much good that surely God must have called them." The other day a dear man
said to me, "But so many souls have been saved under the
ministry of women preachers. 'By their works ye shall
know them.' Doesn't that prove that God wants women
preachers?" Others have been converted under the ministry of women, and they will be sincerely grieved and
shocked at the thought that women ought not to preach.
They feel that they themselves might have been lost forever had it not been for the preaching of some woman. I
understand their viewpoint, but actually that is not a good
reason for women disobeying the Bible, as I will show you.
Yes, women preachers have done much good and I suppose
have won many souls. But more good would have been
done and more souls would have been won if we had followed God's way instead of man's way in the matter. Wom-
en preachers, in disobeying God, have done more harm than
good. Several things need to be said on this question.

First, God's mercy is so great that He uses us poor, im-
perfect instruments. He uses the blundering effort of many
who do not do things according to His methods, because they
are ignorant of God's plan. Women who have not been

taught what God has said on this matter try to preach. Often they are really saved; they love the Lord wholeheartedly; they long to be used; and God blesses their devotion though He does not approve their disobedience.

For example Roman Catholic nuns have done great good. They have waited on the sick, they have cared for orphan children, they have trained children and they have visited the poor. Many Roman Catholic nuns are most earnest, unselfish creatures, trying to please God. But that does not mean that God wants girls to be nuns. He does not. The Scripture plainly says, "Marriage is honourable in all" (Heb. 13:4). God plainly says that it is a "doctrine of devils" to forbid to marry, as Catholics forbid priests and forbid nuns (I Tim. 4:1-3). God blesses the honest intentions of Catholic nuns and priests, though their system of Catholicism has done infinitely more harm than good, doubtless damning millions of souls by teaching them to look to good works or the Catholic Church, instead of to personal faith in Christ Jesus as Saviour.

Christian Scientists, no doubt, do much good. A woman said to me: "Christian Science has certainly satisfied my heart. I have regained my health, I have learned peace of mind and I have great happiness since I took up 'science.'" I think there is no doubt that many people are healed in connection with the teaching of Christian Science and many others attain peace of mind. That is partly because, no doubt, God is pitiful and merciful and if earnest, believing hearts cry out to God, He hears them and blesses them, though He does not approve the system nor the doctrines involved. I have no doubt that Christian Science in denying the blood atonement, denying the fact of sin, denying the essential deity of Christ, denying the need for a new birth, is damning literally hundreds of thousands of souls. It does some good, but it does infinitely more harm. If Christian Science had never been invented by that many-times-married woman preacher, Mrs. Eddy, there would have been more prayers answered, more souls saved, infinitely greater good done.

The lodges, I know, teach men to subdue their passions, to exercise brotherly love, to help each other in trouble. The lodges have helped some men to live better moral lives, and I have known rare cases in which the lodge ties were used to win souls. Many, many earnest, upright men strive to help themselves and help others to a higher, nobler life by the lodges. Yet many Scriptures expressly forbid Christians to yoke up with unbelievers in the lodges. And the lodges, I have no doubt, as a general thing, deny the deity of Christ, deny the need for a new birth, and deceive millions of people who think they are saved without being born again. The lodges do good, but they do infinitely more harm.

So it is with women preachers. They do good, but how much harm they do! First, the rise of women preachers has meant the rise of multiplied sects of people with false doctrines of every kind. The Fox sisters and Spiritism, Mrs. White and Seventh Day Adventism, Mrs. Mary Baker Eddy and Christian Science, Mrs. Filmore and Unity, Mrs. Aimee Semple McPherson and the so-called "Foursquare Gospel," Pentecostalism and its vast majority of women preachers with the blight of sinless perfection doctrine, radical emotionalism, "speaking in tongues" and trances, its overemphasis on healing that leads thousands to despair after false pretenses of healing—these things surely should warn us that there is infinite harm in women preaching. I have been amazed to see in literally scores of cases that the husbands of women preachers were not saved and their children were unsaved. Unsaved men in such cases are usually scornful, bitter, hardened. Women preachers have given the world an impression that Christians are emotionally unstable, that preaching is a racket. Doubtless, thousands of men have been kept out of the ministry because the ministry, as it is known to the people, does not appeal to the best in strong men. And the churches have become so effeminate, so engaged in inconsequential social affairs, so given to display of clothes, so encased in sense-pleasing formalism, that they do not appeal generally to vital business men, strong, earnest robust men.

You can be sure that the kind of Christianity that produces Aimee Semple McPherson does not at the same time produce Spurgeons, Finneys, Moodys, Torreys and Chapmans. Feminism in the churches is a blight that has grieved God and made ineffectual His power and it has disillusioned the people and lost their confidence. I have no doubt that millions will go to Hell because of the unscriptural practice of women preachers.

After all, man's plan may seem to us to be as good as God's, but it never works out that way. When the Bible forbids women to preach or usurp authority over men and commands them to be in silence and obedience in the churches, then that is the best way to win souls, and that way will turn out with the greatest glory to God and the greatest blessings to men. If you would rather believe your reason than the Bible, you may believe in women preachers. But some day you will find out that your poor, fallible, human reason is not as wise as the wisdom of God revealed in His Word.

Some people say, "Women must be called of God to preach because some of them have done much good." But Christians are never to judge by appearances when they contradict the Word of God. God's Word plainly teaches that sometimes God tests His people, whether they will obey Him by letting wicked things apparently succeed. For example, Deuteronomy 13:1-4 gives us clear warning on this subject. It says:

"If there arise among you a prophet, or a dreamer of dreams, and giveth thee a sign or a wonder, And the sign or the wonder come to pass, whereof he spake unto thee, saying, Let us go after other gods, which thou hast not known, and let us serve them; Thou shalt not hearken unto the words of that prophet, or that dreamer of dreams: for the Lord your God proveth you, to know whether ye love the Lord your God with all your heart and with all your soul. Ye shall walk after the Lord your God, and fear him, and

*keep his commandments, and obey his voice, and ye shall
serve him, and cleave unto him."*

Here God tells us that He allows false prophets and
dreamers to give a sign or wonder, and allows the sign or
wonder foretold really to come to pass. But He expressly
commands that if the signs come to pass, "Thou shalt not
hearken unto the words of that prophet, or that dreamer of
dreams: for the Lord your God proveth you, to know
whether ye love the Lord your God with all your heart and
with all your soul." So, no doubt, God has allowed disobedience to prosper temporarily and outwardly for a time
so that His people would be proved as to whether they really loved the Lord 'with all their heart and with all their
soul.' People who go by appearances and what seems to
them to be blessed of God, ignoring God's plain Word, do not
love God with all their hearts and all their souls.

This is an old, old theory advanced by Satan that it is all
right to do evil just so good comes of it. And the Lord gives
the plain rule for every Christian to follow in such cases.
Where the Lord has seemed to bless a prophet who is not
true to God, still you are not to listen to the false prophet's
teachings because of his apparent success, but rather, "Ye
shall walk after the Lord your God, and fear him, AND
KEEP HIS COMMANDMENTS, AND OBEY HIS VOICE."
What God wants Christians to do is to obey His voice, keeping the commandments of His Word, the Bible.

The apparent success of some women preachers is no excuse for disobeying the plain teaching of the Word of God.

(2) Another argument for women preachers is, "But
some women say they have a divine call to preach."
Yes, women sometimes say they are called to preach.
And sometimes it is true that God has been dealing
with their hearts and earnestly urging them to a
complete surrender and to give themselves to soul
winning. Women often, out of a real love for God
and a love for lost souls, give themselves to the ministry.
But they misunderstand God's call. God does want women
to win souls. He wants women to teach women, to teach

children, to do personal soul winning with men and women and children. I know one earnest Christian woman who never makes a talk in public (except a brief testimony of praise in testimony meetings) and who has never stood in a pulpit, never tried to expound the Scripture to a congregation and never taught a mixed class. And yet this woman won 360 souls in one year, and I believe she will have thousands of souls to her credit in Heaven, far more than the average preacher. God called her—but He did not call her to preach, contrary to the Bible. He called her to win souls, person to person, house to house, anywhere and everywhere she could. I say, women, earnest, good women, sometimes misunderstand the call of God.

And other times women say they are called to preach when they want the publicity, the fame, the applause of the crowd. Some men are in the ministry for selfish reasons. Some women are in the ministry for the same selfish reasons. And in the case of some men, and some women alike, no doubt, their motives are mixed. That is, they want to win souls, but they also want fame and honor. So some women honestly want to win souls, but they want to be in the public eye, too. And instead of personal soul winning and fitting into God's plan, subject to their husbands and other men in authority in the church, they want to preach. But the Holy Spirit who wrote the Bible does not contradict the Bible when He talks to a woman's heart. God does not call women to be pastors or evangelists, or to teach men, or to have places of authority over men in the churches.

(3) Sometimes women hotly say, "But that is unfair! Not to allow women to preach is unfair discrimination."

The answer to that is easy. First, when did you earn anything from God? What did any man, or woman either, ever do to deserve to be called to preach? To call God unfair about that is wicked, unreasonable, rebellious! It is only God's grace that keeps all of us out of Hell and why should any of us rebel against God's place for us in His work?

In the second place, it is no more unfair that God forbids women to preach than that He forbids most of the men in the world to preach. In a local church, not all the men can be pastor. Did God discriminate against every other man in the world when He called me to preach? Is it unfair that God in His great mercy calls some men to preach and leaves others to do personal soul winning, and not to be official leaders in authority over the churches? This cry comes from a rebellious will to rule and not from that meek and quiet spirit which in the sight of God is of great price. After all, the gospel is the Lord's and not ours, and He has chosen His own plan of getting it out. He does not give every man the same position and the same authority. And He does not give any woman the place of a pastor or evangelist or teacher of men or any place of authority over men, as He expressly says. And obedient-hearted Christians are glad to take the way that God has plainly outlined in His Word.

The Bible does not forbid women to pray, to sing, to testify. It does clearly forbid them to teach or preach or take authority over men. It has sometimes been wisely said that women may teach women and children, and they make up three quarters of the population of the earth. What more could any woman ask?

(4) Another objection is, "But women missionaries preach and often teach men. Would you have women missionaries come home?"

Well, God's Word has very careful instructions that cover the mission work as well as the work at home. Let us remember that missions is not a modern invention. In the New Testament, for instance, there were Missionary Paul, Missionary Silas, Missionary Barnabas, Missionary Timothy, and many others. In fact, nearly all of the Book of Acts is a mission story, telling how soul winners went among the heathen and preached the gospel to people who had never heard it before. So missionaries should follow the same rules laid down in the New Testament which all Christian workers ought to follow. There is a place for women missionaries as soul winners, as teachers of women and children, as wives of good men. God needs women in China just as much as He needs women in America, no more and

no less. And there is no more reason for a woman missionary to violate the command of God, "I suffer not a woman
to teach, nor to usurp authority over the man, but to be in
silence" (I Tim. 2:12), than there is for a woman in America
who wants to preach in violation of God's command.

If you say that a large percentage of missionary work today is done by women, and that women missionaries have
won many souls while they violated God's rule about wom-
en preaching to and teaching men, then I suggest that you
remember the mission work in the New Testament. In Bible
times, using Bible methods, missionaries had more souls
saved than people do in modern times using modern, unscriptural methods. Some people believe that God's work
would greatly suffer if they did not think up new and unscriptural ways to do God's work. Actually, the contrary
is true. God's work suffers greatly because we do not believe His Word and do not use His methods and His message.
If in the New Testament times they did not need women
preachers in the churches, we do not need them now. If
New Testament mission fields did not need women preachers, then modern mission fields do not need women preachers today. And it is the same kind of sin to take modern
and unscriptural *methods* to China as it is to take a modern
and unscriptural *message*.

The deputation work of great missionary societies has
suffered greatly at the hands of women missionaries. If
godly, Spirit-filled men, manly men, should go to the
churches with the appeal that those whom God has called
for His work should come prepared for toil and sweat and
blood and tears, it would do infinitely more for the mission
cause than the prattle about dress and customs and food,
with stereopticon slide pictures of quaint heathen groups
presented so often by women missionaries, largely to groups
of women and children. We have debased the cause of foreign missions by not keeping it on the high, vigorous plane
which the New Testament gives mission work. I do not
mean that women missionaries home on furlough ought not
to speak to groups of women and children about the mission

work; but it certainly violates the command of God for women to speak before mixed audiences of men and women, and to take the pulpit in the churches. And we may be sure that the work of the gospel of Christ among the heathen is not prospered by this sin. However devoted women missionaries are, they still should obey the Word of God, "Let your women keep silence in the churches: for it is not permitted unto them to speak," and again, "I suffer not a woman to teach, nor to usurp authority over the man, but to be in silence."

The question of women preachers, then, is settled by the Bible. First, it is the uniform practice of both the Old and the New Testament that God did not call women preachers. There were no women apostles, no women pastors, no women evangelists in the Bible. And second, the Scripture expressly teaches: "Let your women keep silence in the churches: for it is not permitted unto them to speak" (I Cor. 14:34). And again, "Let the woman learn in silence with all subjection. But I suffer not a woman to teach, nor to usurp authority over the man, but to be in silence" (I Tim. 2:11, 12).

We "moderns" feel that we know so many ways to do the Lord's business that are better than His ways. But when Nadab and Abihu went into the tabernacle, carrying strange fire, not the appointed fire, they were stricken dead by an angry God (Lev. 10:1, 2). When David brought the ark up to Jerusalem on an oxcart instead of the Lord's way, he had trouble, and death struck the man who touched the ark (II Sam. 6:6, 7). And even when the good king Uzziah went into the temple to offer sacrifice, where it was forbidden for anybody but the priest, God struck him with leprosy (II Chron. 26:16-21). And when Miriam the prophetess wanted to usurp authority in religious work, wanted to take a place of leadership like some men had, God struck her with leprosy for her sin (Num. 12:10). And so today there is a curse, a plague of an angry God on churches because we do things our own way instead of the way of God.

May God help us to bring the Lord back into His churches and put Him first. May we take women out of the pulpits. May we take worldliness out of the pew. May God give us grace to take cowardice out of the preachers. And may God give us a heart to put Him first.

There are women doctors, and any woman who can pass the medical course is permitted to be a doctor; yet how few men will call a woman doctor! How few business men on a board of directors would elect a woman as general manager of a big company. How few men would hire a woman boss over other men. The truth is that men know that which is so plain in all nature, that God did not intend a woman to be in authority over men. It is unnatural and inefficient. Then do you wonder that in the modern sissyfied churches the average he-man will have no part? There was never any lack of men to hear the gospel under the bold, strong preaching of Spurgeon, Wesley, Finney, Moody, Torrey and Billy Sunday. And plain, solid, masculine preachers with holy boldness and a John the Baptist type of ministry, have no trouble getting a hearing among men today.

The gospel is blood and fire and iron. We need more than a vaudeville show in the pulpit. We need more than child prodigies and boy preachers and women evangelists in the pulpit if the church is to take its rightful place in society and if the gospel is to be heard with respect and conviction by ungodly sinners. God bless our good women; He has a blessed place of influence and soul winning for them, but it is *not* in the pulpit. The pulpit is a place for the strongest men that we have. The preacher in the pulpit should speak with an authority that is absolutely forbidden a woman to exercise.

Oh, for a new passion in the churches to do things exactly God's way! Then, no doubt, there will be the smile of Heaven upon us and a mighty revival will break out in the land wherever people make Christ the Lord and set out to please Him.

CHAPTER V

BOBBED HAIR, THE SIGN OF WOMAN'S REBELLION AGAINST HUSBAND, FATHER AND GOD

Now at last we come to the question of bobbed hair.

Do not confuse the subject of bobbed hair with the general subject of woman's dress and use of cosmetics. The question of whether a Christian woman bobs her hair is of infinitely more importance than whether she paints her face or her lips or her fingernails.

A Christian woman ought to dress "in modest apparel" (I Tim. 2:9), and that command would make every earnest Christian woman careful not to expose her body unduly to the lustful gaze of evil men, nor to tempt clean-hearted, good men. But we are not discussing the clothes here.

Surely we will all agree that a Christian woman who does not live as the world lives and does not follow the world's ideals should not make too much effort to look like worldly women. Of wicked Queen Jezebel we are told that "she painted her face, and tired her head . . ." (II Kings 9: 30). The Bible does not give detailed instructions about lipstick and rouge and painted fingernails. But the most spiritual Christians among women usually feel that they cannot go to the extremes that worldly women follow in painting the face, in use of lipstick, in plucking the brows, and in other unnatural fads. Great numbers of the most spiritual women feel that to follow such a pattern is worldliness and hinders a Christian woman's influence. Besides, the women of the best taste know that they are only temporary fads and do not aid real beauty.

Yet the Bible does not expressly forbid the use of rouge. Spiritually-minded women should prayerfully consider their influence and try to please God. I cannot speak with Bible authority on the question of painted faces as I can on the question of bobbed hair. As to whether a woman should use paint at all, or how much, she must try to have the Spirit's leadership and not be offensive; the Bible gives no explicit directions. But on the matter of bobbed hair, the Bible is so clear that nothing is left to a woman's judgment as to whether she should have bobbed hair or long hair. The Bible expressly teaches that a woman should have long hair and gives a very beautiful and forceful reason for the command.

Let us examine again I Corinthians, chapter 11, verses 3 to 9:

" *3 But I would have you know, that the head of every man is Christ; and the head of the woman is the man; and the head of Christ is God. 4 Every man praying or prophesying, having his head covered, dishonoureth his head. 5 But every woman that prayeth or prophesieth with her head uncovered dishonoureth her head: for that is even all one as if she were shaven. 6 For if the woman be not covered, let her also be shorn: but if it be a shame for a woman to be shorn or shaven, let her be covered. 7 For a man indeed ought not to cover his head, forasmuch as he is the image and glory of God: but the woman is the glory of the man. 8 For the man is not of the woman; but the woman of the man. 9 Neither was the man created for the woman; but the woman for the man.*"

The above Scripture tells us that since the man is the head of the woman, and there is a fundamental difference between men and women, that difference should be symbolized in the ways men and women wear their hair.

Throughout the Bible it is stressed that men and women are different. A man is not like a woman. A woman is not like a man. It is a sin for a woman to try to appear like a man, and it is likewise a sin for a man to try to appear like a woman. God has one place for a man and a different place for a woman. For this cause in Deuteronomy 22:5 we are commanded: "The woman shall not wear that which pertaineth unto a man, neither shall a man put on a woman's garment: for all that do so are abomination unto the Lord thy God." It is a sin for women to appear masculine. It is equally a sin for men to appear effeminate. In fact, I Corinthians 6:9, 10 names some of the unrighteous that "shall not inherit the kingdom of God." And among the adulterers and fornicators and drunkards and thieves and covetous and extortioners, God put the *effeminate*. To be effeminate is a horrible sin in God's sight. And the first sin with which God chided Adam, after the fall, was this: "Because thou hast hearkened unto the voice of thy wife . . ."

I say, God has given man one position and woman another position and this difference in their position should be shown by men having short hair and women long hair. "Every man praying or prophesying, having his head *covered,* dishonoureth his head. But every woman that prayeth or prophesieth with her head *uncovered* dishonoureth her head: for that is even all one as if she were shaven" (I Cor. 11: 4, 5). And verse 6 continues: "For if the woman be not covered, let her also be shorn: but if it be a shame for a woman to be shorn or shaven, let her be covered."

Man is made in the image of God. God is a masculine God. The masculine pronoun is used of God everywhere in the Bible. That foolish and unscriptural title given by a woman preacher, Mrs. Mary Baker Eddy, "Our Father-Mother God," dishonors God. God is not effeminate. God is not feminine, but masculine. And man is made in the image of God. On the other hand, a woman is not made so much in the image of God, but in the image and as a mate to man. So the Scripture says: "For a man indeed ought not to cover his head, forasmuch as he is the image and glory of God: but the woman is the glory of the man."

Blessed is the woman that remembers this; her glory is in being a help to a man, and in submission to her husband or her father. And long hair is the mark of this submission, the mark of this femininity.

A man should not pray or prophesy with his head covered. That would dishonor his head, says the Scripture. Men instinctively know that it is shameful to wear hats in public service, and reverent men remove their hats when

The author's daughter, Mary Lloys, when she was fourteen.
"If a woman have long hair, it is a glory to her"—I Cor. 11:15

they pray. Likewise, men instinctively know that they ought not to have long hair. A man has short hair, and this symbolizes the fact that he can approach Jesus Christ freely and that he takes the responsibility as the head of his home.

On the other hand, a woman who prays or prophesies with her head uncovered dishonors her head. Now look at verse 15 and you will see plainly that God is not talking about a woman wearing a hat or veil. Verse 15 says: "But if a woman have long hair, it is a glory to her: for her hair is given her for a covering." A woman, when she prays, should have a covering, some symbol that marks her as an obedient and surrendered wife or daughter. Her long hair is given her for a covering, and a woman who does not have her head covered in that way dishonors her head. And verse 6 says that it is a shame for a woman to be shorn, and she ought to be covered. This symbolic covering or veil for a woman is long hair. Long hair is a mark of a woman's womanliness in God's sight, and is plainly given her for that express purpose, as verse 15 says.

Some people think that there are no religious ceremonial symbols for New Testament Christians, but they are wrong as just a moment's thought will show you. Baptism is a precious ceremony, picturing the burial and resurrection of our Saviour. It pictures also that the believer in Christ is counted dead with Christ and is raised up to live a new life. It pictures also the blessed hope of the resurrection from the dead, when all the bodies of the saints will come out of the graves. Baptism pictures a precious truth and is so important in its doctrinal teaching that it must not be ignored.

Likewise, the Lord's Supper or Memorial Supper of bread and the fruit of the vine pictures the broken body and the spilled blood of our Saviour, and the Lord Jesus said, "This do in remembrance of me." The Christian thus by partaking of the bread and grape juice pictures the fact that he has partaken of the body and blood of the Lord by trusting Him for salvation.

In ordination of ministers and deacons, the ordaining council or presbytery lays hands on the head of the candidates, symbolizing that these are to receive authority from God, and more than that, that they need to receive and should receive the power of the Holy Spirit.

James 5:16 tells us that the elders of the church are to be called in cases of sickness and are to anoint the sick with oil in the name of the Lord and that the prayer of faith shall save the sick. Oil symbolizes the work of the Holy Spirit, whose miracle-working power we have a right to claim when God gives the faith for it.

Thus you see that New Testament Christians have a number of symbols, ceremonies which have a precious and holy meaning. And we must add to this list the symbol of short hair for men, and long hair for women. Men wear short hair as a sign that they take their responsibilities as made in the image of God and as rulers over their households. Women are to wear long hair as symbols of their submission to husband and father, taking their place with meekness as women surrendered to the will of God and subject to the authority God places over them.

In this passage of Scripture, comparing verse 6 with verse 15 we find that God mentions three ways for a woman's hair to be worn. It may be "shaved," that is, all cut off, or "shorn," that is, cut with shears or scissors, or it may be "long." Women often sincerely inquire how long hair must be to be counted long. The answer is that if it is not shaven and not shorn, it is long. God does not say how many inches long hair should be, but simply indicates that it should be left uncut, the symbol of a devout Christian woman who is not in rebellion against God and against her husband.

CHRISTIAN WOMEN SHOULD WEAR LONG HAIR
"BECAUSE OF THE ANGELS"

In the eleventh chapter of I Corinthians we find a remarkable teaching which ought to stir the heart of every woman. The Lord says, "For this cause ought the woman to have power on her head because of the angels." The word *power* here means authority. The Revised Version says, "A symbol of authority on her head." A woman ought to have a symbol of her husband's authority or her father's authority on her head. That is, a woman should wear long hair to indicate that she is submissive to the authority God has put over her. And this special reason mentioned here for a woman having long hair is that angels look on, and for their sakes a woman needs to have long hair!

The angels of God are all about us. People often think of angels as remaining in Heaven and only coming to earth on rare occasions to bring some message. But that is not true. The chief business of the angels is on earth, not in Heaven. Hebrews 1:13, 14 shows that the angels are not sitting on the right hand of God but "Are they not all ministering spirits, sent forth to minister for them who shall be heirs of salvation?" The angels are ministering spirits, sent to wait on us who will one day fully inherit our salvation.

Angels appeared to Jacob on a ladder reaching from Heaven, as the young man slept with his head on a stone, and "behold the angels of God ascending and descending on it." Angels whose work is on earth ascend to Heaven evidently to make report, but they descend again to take up their work. When Elisha, the prophet of God, was at Dothan, unseen to other eyes the angels of God made a ring of fire around the city with their "horses and chariots of fire" (II Kings 6:17). The Lord Jesus says about little children, that "their angels do always behold the face of my Father which is in heaven" (Matt. 18:10). And Psalm 34:7 says that "The angel of the Lord encampeth round about them that fear him, and delivereth them."

So angels are all round about us. And they are surpassingly concerned about our lives! How strange that only rarely do people see them! Our eyes are blinded! We think that the other world, the unseen world and spirit beings are far, far away, but that is not true. And how angels do listen when a woman kneels to pray! For the sake of angels who always hover near, Christian women should especially be careful to have long hair—"because of the angels," the Scripture says.

How are angels concerned about a woman's hair? I

think that not only would angels be grieved by this mark of rebellion against husband or father and against God, but angels would be tempted, likewise, to rebel.

We know that some angels are fallen angels. I understand the Bible to teach that Satan himself was Lucifer, an archangel, who became ambitious and rebellious and said, "I will ascend into heaven, I will exalt my throne above the stars of God" (Isa. 14:13). He wanted to be like God (Isa. 14:14), and was not willing to be subject, just as many women want to be equal to their husbands instead of being subject to them. And Satan fell. So a great group of angels fell, too. Revelation 12:4 may suggest that a third of the angels fell. I do not know how many. But actually, these angels are now chained in darkness, waiting judgment (II Peter 2:4). Angels can fall, and in the past angels have fallen into sin.

And this is especially sad when we remember that Christ never became an angel and did not die for angels. There is nothing said in the Bible about the redemption of fallen angels. If God has any plans for saving angels, He has not revealed them to us.

What sins did angels commit when they fell? They did not get drunk. They did not commit adultery, for it seems that angels are sexless beings who neither marry nor are given in marriage (Matt. 22:30). We suppose that heavenly angels, accustomed to the beauty and glory of Heaven, are never covetous. No, the sin of angels is the sin of rebellion. I suppose that no angel ever fell except by the horrible sin of rebellion against the will of God.

Thus, when a woman with bobbed hair and a rebellious heart comes to pray, angels who hover near and see her head and see her heart are tempted to sin; are tempted to commit the sin which such women commit, the sin of rebellion against authority. Because of the angels, every woman should wear long hair and be careful that she does not have a rebellious heart lest she should be a curse to the angels God has sent to be our ministers and guardians.

How strange and yet how touching is the thought that

the beloved angels of God around us could be led to sin by our sin!

From this Scripture it becomes evident how hateful is the symbol of bobbed hair to God. And how it reveals the stubborn self-will of modern woman who is no longer willing to take the place God assigned to godly women. I beseech the reader that if you are a woman you consider how God must feel toward this mark of rebellion, bobbed hair. No wonder that I Corinthians 11:5 says that every woman with a bobbed head has a dishonoured head. And I Corinthians 11:6 says that it is a shame for a woman to be shorn or shaven and that she ought to have a covering. And I Corinthians 11:15 says that long hair is given her for this covering.

Long Hair, the Glory of a Woman

I Corinthians 11:11-15 says:

"11 Nevertheless neither is the man without the woman, neither the woman without the man, in the Lord. 12 For as the woman is of the man, even so is the man also by the woman; but all things of God. 13 Judge in yourselves: is it comely that a woman pray unto God uncovered? 14 Doth not even nature itself teach you, that, if a man have long hair, it is a shame unto him? 15 But if a woman have long hair, it is a glory to her: for her hair is given her for a covering."

Let no woman be discouraged because God insists that she shall take a place of subjection and wear the mark of humility and femininity on her head. It is true that the man was created first and then woman created second as a helpmeet, as we were told in verses 8 and 9 above. But dear woman, be not grieved. Long hair is not a shameful mark. Rather, it is a mark of glory. God did not mean for the man to be without the woman (v. 11). Both are necessary. Each one is a complement for the other. Each is dependent upon the other. And God's way is the fitting and beautiful and happy way.

Elizabeth Rice, age 14

Since the meaning is made clear in this passage, I suggest that you take heed to verse 13, "Judge in yourselves: is it comely that a woman pray unto God uncovered?" If bobbed hair means rebellion, if it means a sinful disregarding of a woman's place, if it flaunts that rebellion in the face of the angels of God and tempts them to sin, if it means that a woman is trying to be masculine and is giving up her feminine beauty, then doesn't even nature itself teach you that it is comely for a man to have short hair and a woman to have long hair? And isn't it clear, as verses 14 and 15 say, that long hair for a man is a shame, but for a woman, it is a glory to her?

If women only knew the charm and beauty of long hair to intelligent men and the reverence it inspires for godly women, they would never cut their hair. I look back with the tenderest emotion to the vision of my mother, even on her bed in her last sickness, when long braids of black hair lay on her pillow beside her head. It is sweet to believe that I will see my mother again, as a womanly woman with beautiful long hair. I remember with what pride I saw my bride take down her long hair and brush it. To me even then, though I did not know the Scriptures on this subject, long hair was a symbol of something holy and beautiful in women, something tender and pure. Long hair in any woman makes her appear more womanly and there is a sweet and pure charm for men in the feminine beauty of long hair.

One of the most touching stories in the Bible is that given in Luke 7:37, 38:

"And behold, a woman in the city, which was a sinner, when she knew that Jesus sat at meat in the Pharisee's house, brought an alabaster box of ointment, And stood at his feet behind him weeping, and began to wash his feet with tears, and did wipe them with the hairs of her head, and kissed his feet, and anointed them with the ointment."

How Jesus seems to have delighted in having His feet wiped with the long hair of this woman's head. The Lord Jesus forgave and saved this woman, but she could never have given this beautiful mark of her devotion and surrender and love, drying her tears from His feet with her hair, if she had been a modern woman with bobbed hair. Don't you think this story shows the Saviour was pleased with her long hair? I can imagine that even after the Saviour was crucified, this woman, saved from a life of sin, would brush her long hair happily and remember that with it she had had the joy of wiping the feet of the Saviour the day her sins were forgiven. Long hair is a woman's glory.

I well remember knowing one lost man who scorned the attempts of a number of loved ones to talk to him about his poor, lost soul but who listened with most reverent respect to his sister-in-law, because she had long hair and he believed her to be the modest and purehearted woman that her hair indicated. He did not know the Scriptures, but he knew instinctively that God meant for a woman to be womanly. Just as crude and unlettered men seem to know they should take off their hats when they enter public worship or when people pray, so they likewise instinctively know that women, to keep their place as modest and feminine women, should have long hair.

Many a woman feels this though she cannot put it in words. I suppose that literally scores of women have told me how, when they heeded the dictates of fashion and finally had their long hair cut off, they looked in the mirror and wept inconsolably at their loss. And well they might! The Bible says that long hair is a woman's glory and to have it shorn is her shame and dishonors her head.

The modern woman wonders why now she must chase a beau down, as her mother never did. The modern woman wonders why men do not rise up on the streetcar to give her a seat. The modern woman wonders why some men feel so free to curse in her presence, and to use language that no respectable woman of the past generation ever heard. Yes, the modern, masculine, pants-wearing, cigarette-smoking, bobbed-haired woman has fallen from her pedestal. She is not reverenced by men as her beautiful and modest mother was.

These days men have come to feel that if a woman will

not fill a woman's place, she shall not have a woman's protection and respect and reverence. Men desert their wives as never before in the world. Very few men nowadays feel reverently about a woman's body. Boys who have dates with these bobbed-haired, smoking, strong-willed, modern girls, expect to kiss them and fondle them as they please, or to kick them out of the car to walk home. The man who marries a modern woman these days marries a woman who expects to vote like a man, smoke like a man, have her hair cut like a man, and go without restrictions and without chaperons and obey nobody. A man who marries such a woman, I say, does not expect to support her. The modern girl is very often expected to work and help make a living.

In I Peter 3:7 husbands are commanded to give "honour unto the wife, as unto the weaker vessel." When women cease to admit that they are the weaker vessels as God's Word says they are, then they lose this honor that men through the centuries have delighted to give to women. How many men now rise to give a seat on the streetcar to a woman? I am told that not long ago a man on the streetcar rose and offered his seat to a woman, and she was so surprised she fainted! When she recovered consciousness she said, "Thank you!" and then he fainted! I say, the honor, the deference, the courtesy, the protectiveness that practically all men, good and bad, once offered to good women, has almost disappeared!

I remember a time when every good woman, that is everyone who was not a harlot, received the utmost respect from practically every man. In circles of only ordinary culture, the worst men never took God's name in vain in the presence of women, and no gentleman ever smoked in the presence of a woman without her express permission. But today the masculine, rebellious woman has lost the reverence and respect good women once inspired in all men.

Oh, women, what you have lost when you lost your femininity! When you bobbed your hair, you bobbed your character, too. Your rebellion against God's authority as exercised by husband and father, has a tendency, at least, to lose you all the things that women value most. If you want reverence and respect from good men, if you want protection and a good home and love and stedfast devotion, then I beg you to take a woman's place! Dress like a woman, not like a man. Have habits like a woman. No woman ever gained by cursing and smoking and beer drinking and a rowdy life. And if you want God to especially bless you when you pray, then have on your head a symbol of the meek and quiet spirit which in the sight of God is of such great price.

Is it a sin for little girls to have bobbed hair? The Bible does not separately discuss that question as far as I know. But a girl should be subject to her father and should have the "symbol of authority" on her head. In our own home I felt that since my girls would grow to be women, they had better begin to feel like women and act like women. So all of my six daughters have long hair. And how beautiful it is! And when the matter is settled while they are young, and the character is fixed into the lines of womanly behavior and womanly thought and ideals, then I do not expect a great clash and struggle after they are women. Why should not girls be taught that long hair is a glory, as God has said? Why should they not revel in the thought of being women, wives and mothers? Though the Bible gives no separate teaching about girls, it implies clearly that the same rules would apply. For instance, Numbers, chapter 30, mentions a daughter's responsibility to her father, along with a wife's responsibility to her husband. And in this entire passage of I Corinthians 11, the Scripture does not say *wife* but it says *woman*. It does not say *husband*, but it says *man*. God is dealing with women as women on the question of bobbed hair, and they ought to take the woman's place, whether they are married or unmarried.

"If Any Man Seem to Be Contentious"

This passage on bobbed hair, I Corinthians 11:1-16, ends with this statement:

"But if any man seem to be contentious, we have no such custom, neither the churches of God."

On the matter of submitting to authority, there are frequently those who "seem to be contentious." Self-will dies hard, even in a Christian. We want our own way. Some of the Christians who were servants and slaves thought that now they were Christians they need not obey their masters. And children felt that now they were saved, they were equal to their parents. Citizens felt that they now need not obey their heathen rulers, and wives naturally felt themselves equal to their husbands. Were they not saved just the same way? Were not all members of the body of Christ alike? But to such people the Lord plainly gave command as you see in Colossians 3:18-25, Ephesians 5:22—6:9 and elsewhere. No doubt some wives wanted now to cut their hair and act like men. And perhaps some men encouraged it. Some men do now. But to all such Paul said, "But if any man seem to be contentious, we have no such custom, neither the churches of God." No custom of bobbed hair was allowed for women in New Testament churches. Paul, the apostle of the Gentiles, who had more to do with founding churches and their control than any other man who lived, plainly said that this custom was never recognized and never allowed. Bobbed hair is unscriptural and the idea of it was utterly repugnant to New Testament Christianity.

There are many alibis and excuses for bobbed hair. I mention some of them.

(1) "Bobbed hair is so much cooler," so I have heard many a woman say. But then I have seen the same woman wearing a fur coat in warm weather. The fur coat was in style and long hair was not in style. Was that the real basis of the bobbed hair? I simply say that God knew what He was doing and the best women in the world for many centuries have not found long hair too hot for comfort. It is an insincere alibi.

(2) "Long hair makes my head ache," so some women whose health is not good tell me. But it is a strange thing that in the years when long hair was counted beautiful and no women had appeared with bobbed hair, women would go

through any kind of pain to have long hair. I remember when my dear mother had typhoid fever and most of her hair came out. She saved the hair very carefully and had it made into switches, and wore those switches until her own hair naturally grew out thick and full again! And that was a well-known custom in those days. Women who endure operations to have their faces lifted, who have eyebrows plucked, who spend miserable hours getting permanent waves and go through so many discomforts for so-called modern beauty will not be taken very seriously when they say that they have their hair cut because long hair brings discomfort. The truth of the matter is, the same women who wear short hair go to an infinite amount of trouble and annoyance in order to "keep up with Lizzie" and keep in style. It is doubtful if women living a normal life and trying to please the Lord in this matter will ever fail to find some way they can wear long hair very comfortably if they really try to do it for Jesus' sake. And if it is uncomfortable to wear long hair, why then a little discomfort is not much to suffer for Jesus, who suffered so much for us, and who has done so much to lift woman from the awful degradation which heathen women suffer. Women owe enough to Christ to suffer some discomfort if need be. But that is not the real reason women cut their hair. The real reason is that they want to follow the styles.

(3) "But it takes so much time to comb long hair," some women complain. Yet the same women spend hours in beauty shops. They spend time every day patting on creams, applying nail polish or removing it; they spend time in manicures, time in shampoos, in waves, etc. On the average, the women who have bobbed hair spend more time trying to care for their fake beauty than the devout good women with long hair. Again, this complaint was never heard in the days when it was stylish to have long hair. What woman do you know who would not be willing to spend a little time to be, as she thinks, beautiful and in style? This is not a sincere reason but an alibi for those who want to keep up with the outside world.

(4) "But long hair will make me queer," say some women. No, it will not. All through the years some of the most respected and greatly loved women, women in public life even, never looked queer. But if it did make you look queer, then a Christian can afford to be queer in order to be right.

(5) "But my husband wants me to have bobbed hair, and you said for me to obey my husband," some woman says. No, you are mistaken. It was not I who said you were to obey your husband. It was the Lord, and the Lord plainly promised that your husband would be won to God by your obedience (I Peter 3:1, 2), and not that you would be led into sin. And any woman who obeys her husband reverently and lovingly in other matters, and explains her Christian convictions on matters of pleasing God, will find that her husband will not want to lead her into sin. I know that God's way always works, and any Christian woman can have God's help in doing right. If you explain why you should have long hair, and obey your husband in other matters, he will not want you to lose your glory by sinning in having bobbed hair.

After all, these silly alibis are not intelligent reasons for disobeying God's plain command. God says that long hair is a woman's glory, her beauty. The Scripture certainly implies that a woman with long hair is more attractive, more feminine, more likely to be loved. And history bears out that inference. But if there is any reproach to having beautiful long hair, then let the Christian woman bear that reproach. It is the reproach of Christ. If it costs something to be a good Christian, then let us pay that cost gladly. No one ever lost when he suffered something for Jesus' sake.

After all, dear woman, if you are a Christian, if you love the Lord Jesus, if you acknowledge Him as the Master of your life, then His command ought to settle the whole question. To please Him, trusting Him to make it worth while, I would start out to be the kind of woman that this Scripture here pictures. I would, with a surrendered heart, submit myself to the authority God has placed over me, whether of husband or father. I would have a symbol of my

femininity on my head, long hair picturing my submission
to the will of God. When I prayed, I would not be a temp-
tation to the angels nor an affront to God. And I would have
the glory, the feminine beauty, that every true and godly
woman has when she is wholly submitted to the will of God
and when that pure heart and meek and lovely spirit are indicated in the way such a woman dresses and speaks and
lives and wears her hair.

Is it really hard to decide when you know exactly what
the Bible says you ought to do?

CHAPTER VI

THE HORRIBLE SIN OF REBELLION

I hope you have seen by this time that my subject does not primarily deal with anybody's hair, whether a woman's should be long or a man's short. I am really dealing with the question of rebellion against God and His authority. It will be no trouble for you, dear woman, to let your hair grow, if you first settle the real question: Are you willing today to surrender absolutely to the will of God and to His authority in your life? You can be subject to your husband if first you wholly submit to God.

But may I speak here not only to women but to men and to every reader. Will you face this question of surrender today? Will you confess your rebellion and forsake it today and repent of it? Will you start out today to try to follow the will of God? First of all, there is the will of God as expressed in the Bible. Will you today take the Bible as the rule of your life? Will you honestly seek to know the will of God and to do it, as expressed in the precious Word of God?

Perhaps today God speaks to you also by the Holy Spirit. There is some personal leading, some clear path marked out by the Spirit that you ought to take. Or there is some sin that you should give up, or some work you should begin. Will you follow the leading of God, no matter where it leads you? Will you bow your will to His will today? Will you say as the Saviour said to His Father, "Nevertheless, not my will, but thine, be done"?

"The powers that be are ordained of God" (Rom. 13:1). Will you begin today to obey the law of the land, as carefully and meticulously as if God had spoken these laws from Heaven? Will you recognize the authority of God in the government?

It may be that your boss is rough, inconsiderate, perhaps

incompetent. Perhaps you are a Christian and he is not. But will you say today by God's grace, "I will be a good Christian in obeying orders as if they were from Christ"?

Many a young man or woman, many a boy and girl will read this message. You are a Christian, perhaps, but you find it hard to submit to the will of your father or your mother. And yet it is the will of God. The authority of the father and mother is the authority of God. Will you submit to it today? I would pray God to give me such a surrendered heart, and start out to do His will in the home.

In schools, in churches, in business, in homes there should be a new dedication of Christians to lives of obedience. Christians should submit themselves to their own government, to their bosses, to their teachers, to their fathers and to their husbands. It may be, Christian, that God wants something you are not willing to give. When I taught in Wayland Baptist College in Texas, a fine young man, a foreign mission volunteer student, came to me with his problems. He was engaged to be married. I knew the girl and knew him well. He said to me, "What shall I do, Mr. Rice? My girl says that she loves me and wants to marry me, but that she cannot go to China. She says that it would break her mother's heart, and she cannot leave her home and her country even for me. If I will stay in this country she will marry me, but if I go to China I must go alone. What shall I do?"

I knew how he had felt the call of God to go to China. He had told me of his surrender and felt that he knew God had called him to take the gospel to that far-off land. So I said to him, "You don't need me to tell you what to do. I didn't die for you. I didn't save you. I didn't call you to preach the gospel. You need not ask me what to do. I think you already know what you must do if you are going to be happy."

He bowed his head for a time and wept and then he said, "Yes, I know what to do! I want my girl if God is willing for me to have her and if He will turn her heart to go with me to China. But I belong to God and there is no use for me to say that I love Him if I am not willing to do what He says. To give up my sweetheart for China is not as much as Christ gave up for me. I know what to do!"

We prayed together that if it pleased God He would give the girl a willingness to go with him to China, but if not, that he might have courage to go alone, if that was God's will for him.

Does God want something you do not want to give? Maybe you have given up a dear baby that God took away. Perhaps there is a bitterness in your heart, a deadness. Perhaps you have never ceased to resent the loss of the one so dear to you. Oh, dear friend, today give up your will! Bow your head to the will of God and let Him have His way. In the long run you are certain to have such peace and joy as you can never know in disobedience and rebellion.

It may be God has called you to preach. You have in mind a great and happy career. So had I. It may be already that the future seems to promise glowing and wonderful things, success, prosperity, friends or even fame. So it seemed to me that night in 1921 in the Pacific Garden Mission in Chicago. I was a graduate student in the University of Chicago. I had a contract as a college teacher for the following year. The future looked oh, so bright! But when I led a drunken bum to the Lord, God seemed to speak to my heart and to say that that was the way of joy and usefulness for me. And so with some trembling and many doubts and fears, I gave myself up to do the will of God wherever it led me; to poverty, to obscurity, to sickness, to the loss of friends, to a hard life, and then to an obscure grave. I say, I faced it all in my heart, but I took the long look and with all my heart I presented my body as a living sacrifice to God. I said with Isaiah, "Here am I; send me" (Isa. 6:8). Will you surrender to the call of God today? Perhaps God does not call you to preach, but He calls you to come out and be separate. He wants you to leave the worldly ways. He wants you to leave the primrose path you have been traveling. He wants you to come out and be separate and touch not the unclean thing. He wants you to give up certain friends, certain ways of living, and put yourself on the altar as an out-and-out Christian. Is that too hard for you?

It was not too hard for Paul. He called himself the bond slave of Jesus Christ. He said, "None of these things move me, neither count I my life dear unto myself, so that I might finish my course with joy, and the ministry, which I have received of the Lord Jesus, to testify the gospel of the grace of God" (Acts 20:24). There were shipwrecks, beatings, stonings, the hate of his Jewish people, with his life in danger again and again, yet Paul did not waver. He bore in his body the scars of the Lord Jesus. He fought the lions at Ephesus. He lived in chains until their rattle and weight must have been as familiar as the beating of his own heart.

"Paul the aged" lived alone. No wife, no child. He had no time to marry in his eager concern to get out the gospel. In the prison he urged Timothy to come before winter, and "bring the cloke." Paul suffered the loss of all things and counted them dung that he might find the Christ and be found in Him. And it is not too much to ask of any person if they love the Lord Jesus. If you love Him, then keep His commandments, surrender yourself to His dear will.

And in the generations that are gone, people died at the stake and died singing, because they loved the Lord Jesus. Missionaries went to the lepers, expecting to contract the terrible disease themselves, as they did. Missionaries have died in the blackness of Africa or in the burning sands of the South Sea Islands. They have been beheaded in China. They have been shipped to Siberia from Russia. Is it too much to ask of Christians that they submit now to the will of God in every detail?

Rev. Joseph P. Boone, a dear Southern Baptist minister, told me how he struggled with God when it was clear to his soul that God had called him to preach the gospel, to spend his life in soul winning. He had planned to be a lawyer; the prospects for the future were bright. His soul shrank from giving up his rosy dreams. When he analyzed his attitude and found he was in rebellion against the will of God, he

said he was desperately shamed. To think that after God
had saved him, had kept him out of Hell, had given him a
home in Heaven, a new heart and wonderful peace, he
would now refuse to do the will of God about anything.
Convicted of the sin of his rebellion, he went into his room
at Baylor University where he was a student and locked the
door. He said, "God helping me, I will never leave this
room until this question is settled and settled right. Either
they will carry me out in a casket or I will go out of here
surrendered to whatever plan God has for me. He owns me,
body and soul. He deserves the best of my love, my service. He shall have it or I will die before I leave this room!"

He threw himself across the bed and wept out his heart
until peace came and he could say, not only with his submitted will, but with a glad, and voluntary surrender,

> "I'll go where you want me to go, dear Lord,
> Over mountain or plain or sea;
> I'll say what you want me to say, dear Lord,
> I'll be what you want me to be."*

And when he told me the story, he testified that the yoke
of the Lord is easy and His burden light. And he told of the
sweet rest of soul he had found in a life surrendered to the
will of God.

Some person will read this, I am sure, who is unsaved.
You have never taken Christ into your heart to be your Saviour and Lord. You have never repented of your sins. You
have never been born again. You are not a child of God.

And may I ask you why? Have you ever analyzed it?
Do you know why today you are outside the arms of God's
loving mercy? Do you know why He has never kissed away
your tears and forgiven all your sins? Do you know why
you do not have the song of rejoicing in your heart and a consciousness that you are God's own child, with a blessed home
in Heaven, and with a new heart in your breast?

I will tell you why. There is only one thing that keeps
you from God and that is a rebellious heart that is not will-

*Used by permission of Homer A. Rodeheaver, copyright owner.

ing to surrender to Jesus Christ. You remember the Saviour told a parable of certain people who sent word after their lord, "We will not have this man to reign over us" (Luke 19:14). So it is that every person in the world who is unsaved has simply refused to submit his rebellious will, his stubborn heart, to the will of the Lord Jesus.

One day every knee shall bow to Christ and every tongue shall confess that He is Lord, to the glory of God the Father, we are told (Phil. 2:10, 11). That must be sometime. Why not let it be before your soul is damned and lost forever?

John 3:18 tells us that "he that believeth on him is not condemned: but he that believeth not is condemned already, because he hath not believed in the name of the only begotten Son of God." And then we have an explanation of why every soul that ever goes to Hell does so. It is given in the following verses, John 3:19-21, which say:

"19 And this is the condemnation, that light is come into the world, and men loved darkness rather than light, because their deeds were evil. 20 For every one that doeth evil hateth the light, neither cometh to the light, lest his deeds should be reproved. 21 But he that doeth truth cometh to the light, that his deeds may be made manifest, that they are wrought in God."

If you are not a Christian, then the only reason is that in your heart you love your sins and you will not surrender your will to Christ. You will not say to the Lord Jesus as Paul did on the road to Damascus, "Lord, what wilt thou have me to do?"

You can be saved today if you will. The Scripture says, "For whosoever shall call upon the name of the Lord shall be saved" (Rom. 10:13). Jesus promised that "him that cometh to me I will in no wise cast out" (John 6:37). It is not the head that keeps you away from God. It is that stubborn, rebellious will of yours. You know you *ought* to love Him. You plan some day that you *will* love Him. But you still want your own way. I remind you that that sin of rebellion against Christ is the thing that made Satan fall from Heaven, and is the same sin that lands every poor, doomed sinner who does not repent in Hell. Will you repent today?

I hope you who read this will have a heart-searching time. I hope that children will submit themselves anew to their parents. I hope that men who work under bosses will be such Christians that they will submit themselves to their bosses as Christians ought to. I hope that wives will submit themselves to their husbands for Jesus' sake. But oh, the most important thing is that you who read this today and are unconverted will here and now submit yourself to Jesus Christ. Give Him your heart. Surrender your will. Trust Him as your own Saviour and do it today!

When the heart fully trusts in Jesus Christ and takes Him as Lord and Master, then it will be easy to settle whether wives shall obey husbands, and whether women shall have long hair. CHRIST OUGHT TO BE FIRST IN YOUR LIFE! Will you make Him first today?

If you will take Christ as your own Saviour and surrender wholly to Him, I hope you will write me and let me know.

In St. Paul, Minnesota, I closed a Sunday afternoon message on the subject discussed in this book. As I recall, I did not give an invitation, but dismissed the congregation and went into an adjoining room. From the back of the auditorium, a young man, eighteen, who had been breaking his mother's heart with gambling and drinking, came out into the room where I was. With tears running down his face, he held out both hands and said, "Brother Rice, today I am ready to meet my Saviour. I give Him my heart today!" I had been preaching on bobbed hair, but he saw that fundamentally what was wrong in his heart was rebellion against Jesus Christ. Bobbed hair is the sin of rebellion against God and that same rebellion was his sin. And he surrendered there. And that is what is wrong with you if you are not saved. The principal thing is not the hair, it is the heart. When the heart gets right, it doesn't take long to get the hair right. If you surrender with all your soul to Jesus Christ, it will not be hard then to surrender to those whom God has put over you in authority.

I suggest that you have a quiet time alone. Don't you want to close the door to your room and get down on your knees and confess your sins to Christ, and say to Him today as Paul did, "Lord, what wilt thou have me to do"? Trust Him for forgiveness and give Him all of your heart and all of your life. What sweet peace you will have! And what eternal blessings will be yours after taking Christ into your heart as your own Saviour and own Lord.

If you will take Christ as Saviour, will you not write me and tell me so? You may write in your own words, or copy the form of this letter here. But above all, mean it in your heart and tell others and set out to live for God after you have trusted Him as Saviour.

My Decision for Christ

Dr. Curtis Hutson
P. O. Box 1099
Murfreesboro, Tennessee 37130

Dear Dr. Hutson:
I have read the book, *Bobbed Hair, Bossy Wives and Women Preachers*. I see that the heart of all sin is rebellion against God. I have been led to see myself a sinner. Here and now I confess my sin to Christ and surrender to His will. I trust Him to forgive me, and I take Him as my Saviour and my Lord. I claim Him as mine today and by His grace, I will try to live for Him the rest of my days.

Signed _____

Address _____

_____

For a complete list of books available from the Sword of the Lord, write to Sword of the Lord Publishers, P. O. Box 1099, Murfreesboro, Tennessee 37133.